THE
COMMUNICATIONS
GOLDEN HOUR

THE COMMUNICATIONS GOLDEN HOUR

THE ESSENTIAL GUIDE TO PUBLIC INFORMATION WHEN EVERY MINUTE COUNTS

DOUG LEVY

Public Safety Press
Sausalito, Calif.

Published by Doug Levy Communications LLC
1 Harbor Drive, Suite 300
Sausalito, Calif. 94965

ISBN 13: 978-1-7320659-0-1

First printing, April 2018

DEDICATION

This book is dedicated to the tens of thousands of public safety and public health professionals on duty every day who keep our communities safe and to the memory of those who gave their lives in service of others.

The best way to honor these heroes is to continually strive to do better; learn from the good and the bad of past incidents; and plan, test, and train for the inevitable next major emergency.

ACKNOWLEDGEMENTS

This book represents my work and the experience of public information officers in police, fire, health, and other public safety agencies over the past 30 years. Their commitment to protecting lives makes working with them a privilege.

I am especially grateful to the leaders and members of the Public Information Officers section of the International Association of Chiefs of Police. This community constantly shares learnings, disseminates best practices, and helps each other out when an emergency occurs.

My colleagues and team members over the years also deserve credit for living through crisis after crisis and sharing my passion to always do better. From my first ambush interview as a new leader of a fire department outside Baltimore years ago to handling calls from global media in the years since, every public interaction has been a chance to learn.

Creative and consistent encouragement and professional guidance from Alicia Dunams and Laura Allen helped bring this book from rough draft to finished product. Also, Peter Shankman and members of his Shankminds group have been a source of energy, wisdom, and unfiltered reactions.

Thank you also to Tatyana Kanzaveli, who persuaded me to write this book in the first place. My friends Ramon Ray and Adryenn Ashley provided subsequent kicks that got it rolling. Debi Stein's fresh eyes helped bring the final draft to fruition. And, editor Lauren Johnson shaped it all over the past year, adding her own PIO experience to her skilled word crafting.

There also are many other friends, family members, and colleagues who have been patient and wise counselors, reviewers, critics, and cheerleaders throughout the research and writing process. Thank you all.

TABLE OF CONTENTS

Preface   xi

Introduction   1
   Ten Lessons Learned.   2
   Communications Timelines in Action   4
   The Las Vegas Massacre   6
   The Sonoma Wildfire Communications Timeline.   8
   False Alarm: Incoming Missile Alert in Hawaii.   10

Chapter 1: Establish Trust and Demonstrate Authority   13
   The Face of Trust: 20

Chapter 2: The Communications Golden Hour   21
   The Systems Approach to Emergency Communications.   21
   The Communications Golden Hour: Minute by minute   28

Chapter 3: Plan, Practice, Revise…and Tweet   35
   Guidelines for Crafting Your Plan   47
   Answer Three Questions.   47
   Designate Your Team   48
   Define Response/Dispatch Levels   48

Chapter 4: Develop the Right Messengers.   49
   Choosing Your Messengers.   50
   Going Live.   54

Chapter 5: Craft the Right Message   59
   Tailor Messages To Your Exact Community   61
   Elements Of An Effective Emergency Message   63
   Communicating About Science And Health.   75
   Putting It All Into Action: The Single Overriding
      Communication Objective.   80

Chapter 6: Mistakes, Misinformation, and Alternate Facts **83**

Plan and Respond with the Knowledge That
Mistakes are *Always* Possible 83

Think Ahead About How to Talk About Errors
by Your Agency 84

Figure Out Where to Improve 84

Common Root Causes of Mixed-Up Messaging 85

Correct Misinformation—No Matter Where it is From 86

Avoid Ambiguity 87

Reality in the Era of "Alternate Facts" 88

When the Media Messes Up 89

Appendix: Tools and Worksheets **91**

Single Overriding Communications Objective Worksheet 92

Tactical Tools And Logistics 94

Communications Emergency Roles 95

Major Incident Communications Checklist 97

Media Briefing Tips 98

Communications Channels 99

Planning For Extended Incidents 101

About the Author **103**

PREFACE

Communicating about a public safety emergency differs from most other kinds of communications because lives literally depend on what you do. You must be accurate. You must be credible. And, you must be aware of how your audience is going to interpret and respond to whatever you say. While every emergency has its own unique facts and circumstances, there are fundamental principles that improve the likelihood that your messages will get life-saving information to the people who need it.

When the phone call came that October day letting me know that one of the doctors at my medical center was infected with Ebola, I knew that the next 24 hours—no, probably the next 72 hours or more—were going to use every skill that my team and I had learned from our collective decades as public information officers.

As the Ebola story played out in New York City, it proved to be even more of a test of our nation's entire public health system. Fortunately, New York City's public health infrastructure and the people who keep it running were well prepared for an Ebola case. The healthcare part of the equation went well. However, calming the hysteria stoked by breathless television anchors and misinformed politicians required not only constant vigilance, but new approaches to how we communicate about public health or any serious emergency.

Having been involved with front-page news most of my career, leading communications at major medical centers for more than a decade, and working in and with emergency services even longer, gave me the confidence to handle it…but there were many new lessons to be learned. The mass shooting in Las Vegas, the acute hurricane damage in Puerto Rico, and the firestorms in Northern California make this stark reality even clearer.

Everybody knows that social media has transformed the way people get information, but there are many confounding factors, such as literacy, language, and culture. Whether you are managing a weather emergency, a fast-spreading infectious disease, or an active shooter, disseminating accurate information about public safety and public health emergencies has never been more complicated.

But it has also never been more possible.

That's right. Possible.

While we cannot *control* the media or the public's interpretation of facts, public information officers have powerful *influence*. The PIO's task is to prime the pump of credible, sharable information. Public information officers in New York, Atlanta, and throughout the nation adapted to the changing landscape. Now, we know more about what works and what doesn't. So, we must make sure we are prepared to rapidly adapt to whatever happens and however public communications changes.

When a bomb exploded on West 23rd Street in New York in September 2016, NYPD used a new alert system to get urgent warnings to cell phones. Citizens who saw the NYPD alerts spotted the bag that later was found to contain a second device. Because of the alerts, they knew to call 911 instead of touching the suspicious bag. Alerts also were sent a few minutes later to tell people to stay away from their windows while the bomb squad handled and removed the second device. The new tools worked.

This book brings together the latest knowledge about how to communicate in the most challenging situations. It is based on actual communications activities during hurricanes, officer-involved shootings, mass casualty incidents, wildfires, and every other life-threatening emergency of the recent past—and *what* we can do better next time. It includes what my colleagues and I learned from managing communications during the Ebola, Zika, and flu outbreaks as well as our experiences with dozens of other public safety and public health crises that tested our ability to convey safety information when lives were on the line. It also reflects the latest research about human behavior and how and why messages work or fail.

If you are a public information officer, this book will help you better understand how people react in emergencies and how you can influence those reactions to keep people safe. The tactics taught here will help you get the right information to the right people at the right time. This is what protecting the public is all about.

INTRODUCTION

"Precision of communication is important, more important than ever, in our era of hair trigger balances, when a false or misunderstood word may create as much disaster as a sudden thoughtless act."

—James Thurber

Recent events change the scale of our thinking about emergencies and how to communicate about them, but the essential skills for effective emergency public information officers remain as they have always been: the ability to communicate quickly, calmly and accurately.

Life-safety communications require a special combination of skills, resources, and people with the knowledge and experience to adapt what they already know to any new situation—whatever its magnitude.

Powerful new tools help us keep up with the quickening pace of communications, but no technology can replace sound judgment under pressure. Skilled public information officers (PIOs) know what words to use to get urgent facts or guidance to the public fast. The best tools are worthless if the words used are imprecise or ineffective or the messages never reach their intended recipients.

Planning for major incidents no longer can be left to state coordinators or the big city departments. Police agencies with only a few dozen officers have found their communities at the top of the national news because of active shooters or other events. Major incidents are not limited only to major cities. Stacks of guidance documents from the Federal Emergency Management Agency may be useful, but no manuals can take the place of hands-on learning by the people who are front and center when an emergency occurs.

TEN LESSONS LEARNED

One of the most important aspects of emergency planning is to evaluate past incidents and learn what worked and what could be improved. From that, these critical points are underscored:

1. **It can happen anywhere**

    No police or fire department, city or state government, or any other emergency management organization can continue to think, "It won't happen here."

2. **Public information is an essential function**

    A skilled public information officer is every bit as essential as tactical or other operational experts. This duty cannot be assigned ad hoc.

3. **Know your tools**

    New systems, such as the Integrated Public Alert & Warning System (IPAWS) coordinated by the Federal Emergency Management Agency (FEMA) have enormous potential when used properly. Know how to use IPAWS, social media, and any other communications channel before you need to. Have an effective social media strategy planned in advance.

4. **Plan, practice, and revise**

    Thinking through how real emergencies could play out in your community is essential both to formulating effective communications plans and to lining up the resources and knowledge that you will need in any emergency. And, the best plans are meaningless if they exist only on paper. Walk through your responses to each possible scenario and identify the proper channel(s) and messaging for each.

5. **Use multiple channels**

    Even if you primarily use one channel, such as Twitter, emergency messages need to be disseminated on every channel that you have access to. Think ahead about communications methods that are likely to fail in an emergency—and have a backup.

6. **The news cycle never stops**
On social media or broadcast TV, news is live all the time. Even morning newspapers continually publish now. Getting urgent information out fast no longer requires programs to be interrupted or schedules to be changed.

7. **News travels fast; bad news travels faster**
The news media wants to help get safety messages to the public. However, if you don't provide information, reporters will turn to others who may not have good information. And, when there is bad news, put it out proactively. Even a simple, brief acknowledgement that there was an incident and that more details will be forthcoming can go a long way toward keeping the public's trust.

8. **If you don't provide information, others will**
By the time St. Louis County Police Chief Jon Belmar briefed reporters the day after the Ferguson, Missouri officer-involved shooting in 2014, unofficial versions had already turned the narrative of the incident into a global news story. During the Northern California wildfires, officials had to constantly counter misinformation because of confusion about who had authoritative instructions for people in the risk area. "We can communicate so fast, but we can also miscommunicate just as fast," said CalFire Division Chief Todd Derum.

9. **Anticipate mistakes and misinformation**
Every plan must incorporate steps to verify information before it goes out and a process to correct incorrect information that gets out anyway. An errant alert can create its own emergency. Plan for it so you know how to correct it fast.

10. Establish trust and demonstrate authority

Trust gets built over time, but it can be destroyed in minutes. Get to know media, community leaders, and others before there is an emergency. Once a crisis begins, acknowledge people's anxiety and let them know you hear their concerns, even if you have few details to share. This also helps block others from inserting themselves into the story. And, if first responders did something wrong, own it and describe what you are doing to make sure mistakes do not recur.

COMMUNICATIONS TIMELINES IN ACTION

The Northern California Wildfires: Missed Communications

Todd Derum has seen big fires in his lifetime in the fire service. As he sat down for a family dinner early in the evening of Oct. 8, 2017, he noticed the winds picking up and knew it could be a dangerous night. He alerted the crews on-duty to be ready, since the fire threat was as high as it could be … high winds, low humidity, and a lot of dried-out brush that grew in abundance after heavy rains earlier in the year.

Hours later, Derum was in the middle of something that no plan anticipated. What started as small brush fires in open space near Calistoga, Calif., raced over the hills and into the city of Santa Rosa—16 miles away, moving the length of a football field every minute. Even the command post had to abruptly change locations.

By the time the Tubbs Fire and two other large wild land fires nearby were contained, over 110,000 acres burned, 6,957 structures were destroyed, and 44 people died, unable to escape the flames.

Emergency responders had everything working against them that night. The winds knocked down utility lines throughout Sonoma,

Napa, and Mendocino counties. That meant that landline phones and electric power both were out in many places. As the firestorm started, cell phone towers burned along with utility poles, so many of the most vulnerable people had no connection to the outside world. How many people have transistor radios anymore? As it turned out, that was one of the remaining ways people in the fire area could receive information.

Despite the widespread outages, the Sonoma County Sheriff's Office, responsible for emergency management, relied on Reverse 911 and the opt-in Nixle system to get the word out about the immediate danger. Unfortunately, Reverse 911 only works if people have functioning landline phones, and there were only 20,000 people signed up for Sonoma County's Nixle alerts when the fires started. The county population is 500,000.

"Some of the phone lines were down. The cell towers were also impacted. Power was out, so people were not checking their computers," said Derum. The only effective alerts "would have been your neighbors, your dog barking, or police or firefighters knocking on your door."

We will never know how many of the people who died might have gotten out had they received better emergency warnings. However, we know that the warnings that were sent were not enough to get everyone out of danger.

Sadly, some of the people who perished might have gotten out had they known how to open their garage doors when there was no electricity. (Most openers have an emergency cord to disengage the opener when necessary.) At least one death occurred when fire blocked the only road out from a remote hillside home.

The conscious decision not to use IPAWS to trigger cell phone alerts is one that will be second-guessed forever. The sheriff says they did not have the option of targeting only part of the county, and a middle-of-the-night alert to 500,000 people—most of whom were not in danger—might have triggered needless and dangerous panic. What is clear is that county officials had not taken enough steps in advance of fire season to implement new warning systems that they could use, and nobody on duty that night knew enough about the tools that were available.

Crafting a message for IPAWS or any system requires care. With only 90 characters available, giving exact locations is a challenge. If this were to happen again, perhaps this would have worked:

> *ALERT: Huge fire spreading west into Fountaingrove and Coffey Park. Evacuate immediately.*

That's 90 characters.

or,

> *ALERT: Major wildfire spreading rapidly into City of Santa Rosa. Be alert and know your way out.*

It could be followed with a message to sign up for the Nixle alerts, which can be more targeted and nuanced but only reach people who opt-in.

The results in Sonoma and surrounding areas also demonstrate why communicating with people in risk areas must be continually, not just during an emergency. Tell people what to do to prepare and protect themselves and how to keep up with official information. Get your audience familiar with your system for sending alerts.

THE LAS VEGAS MASSACRE

Las Vegas - October 2, 2017

Here is the timeline of communications during the Las Vegas shooting. Las Vegas police focused on responding to the emergency, but also got alerts to casinos and others based on pre-existing emergency plans. By communicating with the nearby casinos and rapidly establishing a perimeter, LVPD officers were able to deal with the emergency scene while casino security managed guests and others and kept them from the scene.

10:05-10:15 PM – Heavily armed man shoots at concertgoers from 32nd floor of Mandalay Bay hotel in Las Vegas.

10:16 PM – First social media posts by witnesses.

10:25 PM – Alert sent to Las Vegas cab drivers to avoid Mandalay Bay area due to "possible 3 shooters." A driver posted this to Twitter almost immediately as other taxi drivers also reported on Twitter what they were seeing or hearing.

10:30 PM – More social media posts from the area, including videos of the crowd and confusion during the gunfire.

10:39 PM – First public message from Las Vegas Metropolitan Police Department on Twitter:

> "We're investigating reports of an active shooter near/around Mandalay Bay Casino. Asking everyone to please avoid the area. #LVMPDnews"

11:58 PM – LVMPD tweet that one suspect was "down."

> "Confirming that one suspect is down. This is an active investigation. Again, please do not head down to the Strip at this time."

12:31 AM – LVMPD tweeted:

> "At this time we do not believe there are any more shooters. More information to come shortly from @Sheriff_LVMPD."

THE SONOMA WILDFIRE COMMUNICATIONS TIMELINE

Sonoma County, Calif. - October 8, 2017

9:22 PM – Vegetation fire reported on Buckingham Drive in Santa Rosa

9:23 PM – Power line problem reported on Mark West Road

9:24 PM – Electric transformer explosion reported in Larkfield neighborhood.

By 10:15 PM, the Sonoma County 911 center was flooded with reports of fallen power lines and fires.

Around this time, about a dozen sheriff's deputies circulated in two rural neighborhoods using sirens and their car public address systems to warn of the fast-approaching blaze. They also knocked on doors to get people's attention.

10:51 PM – Sonoma County sent an "advisory," not an emergency "alert" via Nixle:

> *Multiple fires are reported around Sonoma County. We currently have fires at Mark West Springs and Riebli Rd in Santa Rosa, Shiloh and Conde in Windsor, and Hwy 116 at Fredericks Rd in Sebastopol. Local fire departments are on scene and we will notify you if any evacuations are called for. The strong winds are making these fires difficult. Dispatchers are being overwhelmed by 911 calls on reports of smoke smell. Please only call 911 if you see actual unattended flames.*

11:03 PM – Sonoma County sent a much more urgent message:

> *A wildfire has been reported at Porter Creek Rd at Petrified Forest Rd. Mandatory evacuations have been called for. Our*

deputies are en route to assist Fire and CHP with evacuations. If you live in this area, please be alert for the danger. We are not on scene yet and haven't been able to determine the best evacuation route. Cal Fire says the fire is east of that location and roads are open to both Calistoga and Santa Rosa at this moment. 911 lines are inundated. Please only call for immediate emergencies.

Instructions:

If you live in this area please assess danger, notify neighbors of potential danger. Be advised many trees are down on Calistoga Road. Drive slow and safe.

Additional advisories were sent out about new fires and evacuations. Then the firestorm reached the heavily populated Fountaingrove neighborhood of Santa Rosa.

This message went out via Nixle, again as an advisory not an alert, at 1:22 AM on October 9:

Santa Rosa fire spreading quickly.

The fire from Porter Creek road has spread very quickly and has moved down Mark West Rd to Riebli, Thomas Lake Harris towards Fountaingrove, The fire has also spread to Shiloh Ridge. Mass evacuations are taking place. If in this area, you need to move out. 911 systems are inundated. Please call only if you have an immediate emergency.

FALSE ALARM: INCOMING MISSILE ALERT IN HAWAII

Honolulu - January 13, 2018

The timeline provided by the Hawaii Emergency Management Agency (EMA) and other sources, as reported by the Associated Press, represents a nightmare scenario for anyone who has ever had command of an emergency operations center:

8:05 AM – An unannounced internal drill at shift change was initiated. Worker at the Hawaii EMA mistook a phone call that was part of the drill as an authentic order to send a Civil Emergency Message about an inbound missile. The alert was sent without oversight or review by another person.

8:07 AM – Wireless Emergency Alert sent to cell phones throughout Hawaii:

> *"Ballistic missile threat inbound to Hawaii. Seek immediate shelter. This is not a drill."*

Before alert could be sent, the EMA worker had to respond to computer prompt that asked, "Are you sure that you want to send this alert?"

8:08 AM – EMA director was notified of the false alert.

8:09 AM – EMA director notified Gov. David Ige that the false alert was sent. EMA notified county emergency officials that there was no missile threat.

8:10 AM – EMA director confirmed with the U.S. Pacific Command that there was no missile launch. Honolulu Police Department notified of the mistake.

8:12 AM – EMA canceled the original alert so that it would not appear on cell phones turned on that had been turned off when it was first sent.

8:13 AM – EMA and others notified media and others that the alert was a mistake.

8:20 AM – EMA posted to Twitter and Facebook that the alert was a false alarm. The governor was unable to access his social media accounts.

8:24 AM – Gov. Ige retweeted the EMA's tweet about the false alert.

8:30 AM – Governor posted cancellation notification to his Facebook page. Hawaii EMA confers with FEMA to confirm that sending another Civil Emergency Message to rescind the false notification was the right way to correct the mistake.

8:45 AM – New Wireless Emergency Alert sent:

"False Alarm. There is no missile threat or danger to the State of Hawaii."

After getting authorization from FEMA Integral Public Alert and Warning System, Hawaii EMA issued a "Civil Emergency Message" that the earlier alert was a false alarm. This message was transmitted over local television and radio stations, including a "crawl" at the bottom of TV screens.

9:30 AM – Governor's office issued statement to media.

9:34 AM – Governor's message posted to his Facebook and Twitter accounts.

For information about how actual missile or other Civil Emergency Alerts are supposed to be handled, the National Warning System (NAWAS) Operations Manual is available at http://bit.ly/NAWAS.

Now that you know the most important lessons you need as well as how communications timelines rapidly play out, let's take a more in-depth look at putting these lessons into practice. That way, you can be ready for anything—and any emergency.

Chapter 1

ESTABLISH TRUST AND DEMONSTRATE AUTHORITY

"People don't care how much you know until they know how much you care."

—St. Francis Xavier, Theodore Roosevelt, and many others

Police officers, firefighters, and health professionals have the advantage of being in occupations that people generally consider trustworthy. In fact, while college professors, journalists, politicians, and religious leaders have fallen in Gallup's annual survey, nurses continue to rank as the most trusted professionals…as they have for 15 straight years. Pharmacists, doctors, and dentists are also in the top five, along with engineers. Police were No. 6 in the 2016 survey.

However, the degree to which people trust anyone has slipped, and it is very personal. People tend to trust their own healthcare providers, but they do not trust the health profession—or any profession—in the aggregate. Overall, faith in doctors and other health professionals is about half of what it was in the 1970s, according to one survey. And, if health professionals have government titles, some people will tune out whatever they say.

People often rush to discount warnings and assign blame instead of taking swift action. Every emergency management agency will have trouble getting the public to respond to a real emergency because of Hawaii's errant missile warning or other highly publicized false alarms.

Similarly, people may feel safe in a city where they do not trust the police or vice versa. In recent surveys in New York, more people say they are satisfied with the NYPD than say they trust the NYPD. Trust or satisfaction scores rarely line-up with actual crime statistics.

If you are trying to convince people to do something, especially in a crisis, you need to know whether they trust you before you start communicating. Understanding who people trust when emotions are charged is an essential element to managing any crisis. Many residents of New Orleans ignored calls for evacuation prior to Hurricane Katrina because they simply had no faith in their local government.

Unlike in science or academics, your qualifications as a government authority may not matter. Do not count on unquestioned common sense to apply when you most need it to. When a disaster strikes or another danger looms, people turn to people they trust. You cannot expect people to do what you tell them to do if they do not trust you.

People are much more likely to trust a person they know or have seen before. If there is no personal relationship, trust can be earned by a person who demonstrates that they give accurate information and have empathy for the audience. Those two elements help form credibility. Come across as stiff or cold, and your messages are less likely to penetrate, especially when people are scared.

For emergency responders, the best scenario is when relationships have already been established. If a police chief, public health director, or a mayor already has a good rapport with their community, they start from a better place than a person who has never been seen before. This is why having a known person act as a spokesperson may make sense, even if that spokesperson might not be the natural choice based on expertise or job roles. Or, have a known spokesperson introduce the new person—that helps convey credibility and trustworthiness to achieve the communications goal.

As a public information officer, the best practice is to establish and build relationships before a crisis occurs. Your emergency communicators need to be able to walk into a command center knowing which community leaders are allies who they can call on for help in the middle of the night if necessary to help get the word out fast in an emergency.

However, there are rare times when an unknown person acting as spokesperson has an advantage, such as in controversial situations or when public officials have lost credibility. Michigan's state government did this in Flint, when a police spokesperson from a distant part of the state was sent in to take over communications after health and other recognized officials lost credibility during the contaminated water crisis.

When Ebola was at the top of the news in Fall 2014, even people with advanced degrees panicked, along with nearly everyone else, because celebrities and politicians told them to. It did not matter that the world's actual experts on Ebola were calmly and methodically explaining why hysteria was unfounded. Even two politicians with medical training were among the many who stoked fear instead of conveying grounded facts. Before social media, these voices would have been drowned out by ones vetted by major media. Now, there is no such filter.

When I surveyed a random sample of Americans about who they would turn to for information in an emergency, most people said they would rely on their local police or fire department. That makes sense. But that was about the only place where people agreed.

The data shows that young people want to hear from someone they know in real life—such as a friend or neighbor or family member. Older people look for a uniform and a badge. In the middle are people who may gauge credentials a bit more and turn to news outlets or government agencies directly.

Most importantly, do not discount the news media. Even though journalists suffer from a credibility gap, overwhelming numbers still say they will turn to their local media for updates when a crisis occurs—

even if they do not trust all the information. At the very least, people may turn to the news media to see emergency officials' live briefings.

In addition to differences based on age, differences also exist by region, economic status, and between rural and urban geographies.

The bottom line is that emergency communicators cannot presume that they will automatically be trusted by virtue of their position. PIOs must recognize that some people in their area may need to get urgent messages differently. Before you face an emergency, get to know your audience, who they trust, and why.

The epidemic of skepticism contributes to confusion, and it has enormous consequences in emergencies. In the past, mayors, governors, religious leaders, and health directors could step in front of the cameras with instant credibility. No longer can this be presumed. Trust must be earned and maintained—one by one, in many instances.

If a community does not trust their mayor, or the governor, or the president, or the director of public health, or the doctor, or the TV anchor, who do they trust? The answer could be different from one place to the next, or even within sections of a single town or city.

TRUST TAKES TIME TO BUILD BUT CAN BE LOST IN A MOMENT

Trust is a malleable thing and, particularly with social media, it changes—sometimes rapidly. Somebody who is trusted this week may not be trusted next week. Put out incorrect information, even if unintentionally, and lose the trust that you built up before. When a spokesperson for the operator of a commuter train that crashed in rural Maryland in 1996 said that none of his agency's trains was involved—while live TV showed one in flames—the media stopped calling that agency for information on the deadly accident. Honest mistakes can be forgiven. Whoppers like that or any deliberate misinformation, not so much.

FIND OUT WHO KNOWS THE PEOPLE YOU WANT TO REACH

If you do not have a direct relationship with people you are trying to reach, find out who does. Who are their neighbors? What community leaders may get their attention? In some communities, a local business person may be the most effective conduit for solid information. Pharmacists are in especially good positions to be valuable resources, because they know many people and are almost universally trusted.

BE AWARE OF CULTURAL DIFFERENCES

If you have large groups who speak Spanish or another language besides English, get emergency messages out in their native language—if you can get someone fluent to translate. Recognize dialects and how they may differ from one part of your community to another. In some instances, the effort to communicate in-language is enough to build trust—even if you cannot do all your communication in multiple languages. (Artificial intelligence translations such as Google Translate are helpful but not reliable enough for use in an emergency.)

Other differences, such as socioeconomic and geographic, also influence trust. Higher income individuals tend to trust authority, while people in rural communities have great respect for their neighbors. These are all factors that influence how you craft your messages, which is the subject of Chapter Four.

USE THE TRIANGULATION APPROACH TO CREATE AN "ECHO CHAMBER"

People are more likely to believe information they hear from multiple sources. If an emergency official on television says one thing, a person is going to be reassured if they hear their neighbor echo the same message. If they hear it from a third source, even better.

Just as you need multiple technologies for communications, you need multiple people to amplify your messages. Make sure you can get your urgent key messages to other influencers; that is, the people that some in your community trust: politicians, community and religious leaders, business people, and activists. You need to get messages out to the people sitting next to your actual audience, whether by bumping into them at the grocery store or posting on social media. Who else are they going to talk to? How can you spark those interactions when you need an urgent message to travel fast?

RECOGNIZE AND DEAL WITH DIFFERENT TYPES OF EMERGENCIES IN ADVANCE

Ideally, you have time to plan and develop trust with your audience before an emergency occurs. You can get a pretty good idea if there is a big storm coming or if an emerging infectious disease is showing up. Of course, crimes and fires happen without warning. All the more reason to know your circle of influencers ahead of time.

In the case of an infectious disease risk, communicating effectively at the outset makes your messages when the crisis hits much more believable. In the Ebola outbreak of 2014, one of the things that worked in New York was that the health department got fliers to every healthcare office in the city more than two months before the first Ebola case presented. By that point, every physician's office had information. So, when frantic patients called, even the receptionists could say, "Here is what the health department told us about this disease. Here is what we're doing about it." This made the doctor's office credible, and it made the city health department credible. That is the ideal scenario, but not all emergencies are forecast.

IDENTIFY YOUR COMMUNITY MEMBERS WHO ARE INFLUENCERS

When a sudden emergency occurs, identify all the people that your community members are likely to turn to for information, and make sure that those trusted people have your messages. You want those influencers to rely on you for correct information, but you cannot count on them to come to you unprompted or uninvited.

BUILDING AND MAINTAINING TRUST TAKES TIME, BUT IT IS NOT DIFFICULT

First responders conduct drills with each other and with mutual aid agencies so that they are familiar with each other when they respond to an emergency. PIOs need to know their counterparts in other agencies and get out into the community so that they know people before the alarms sound, too. More people will trust familiar faces or names. In emergencies, people look for "officials" who sound knowledgeable and who are empathetic. The best way to be considered empathetic is to already have connections with your audience.

Know also that name recognition may have little or no relation to whether a person has actual knowledge. We know from elections that an inexperienced candidate with a recognized name is more likely to get votes than highly qualified but unknown people. The same thing works when people ask, "can I trust you?" If they have heard of you before, or if they have seen your face, the answer is more likely to be yes. Above all else, always maintain integrity and be truthful. You may report to a government official, but all public employees are accountable to the public.

THE FACE OF TRUST:

Familiarity

Accuracy

Credibility

Empathy

Chapter 2

THE COMMUNICATIONS GOLDEN HOUR

The Systems Approach to Emergency Communications
Think "TRAUMA":
Trust - Established beforehand.
Rapid - Respond rapidly.
Accurate - Always be accurate.
Understand - Understand your audience.
Measure - Measure your results.
Accessible - You and your messages both need to be accessible.

Communications decisions in the first 60 minutes frequently determine whether your emergency communications succeeds or fails.

The crucial 60-minute window for surviving a traumatic injury was first described in the 1960s, when medics, doctors, and nurses looked for ways to keep people from bleeding to death after being torn apart by shrapnel in Vietnam or mutilated in a car crash closer to home. The answers emerged as they methodically studied factors that contributed to whether a person lived or died after a bleeding injury. Perhaps the most important discovery was that survival depended almost entirely on what happened in the first 60 minutes. That led to the transformation of pre-hospital care into today's modern emergency medical services system.

Emergency physician R. Adams Cowley of the University of Maryland dubbed this the "Golden Hour," a term that helped educate everyone from ambulance crews to surgical teams about the importance of knowing exactly what to do with a severely injured patient—without delay. It also spurred development of trauma systems, which organize emergency medical care in specific ways that are proven to increase likelihood of survival. Trauma patients require coordinated care: from the place where the injury occurred to the hospital that can treat the specific type of injury to the rehabilitation facility that promotes successful recovery. Any one part of the system that fails jeopardizes success.

Every day around the world, trauma systems with skilled personnel and resources save people with injuries that would have meant certain death fewer than 50 years ago. Organizing the medical response so that definitive care can be delivered within that Golden Hour has saved countless lives.

THE GOLDEN HOUR WORKS FOR COMMUNICATIONS, TOO

Those of us trying to get life-safety information to the public in emergency situations can learn from what Dr. Cowley did in Baltimore 50 years ago. Just as with emergency medical care, communications decisions made before the first emergency alert goes out and within the initial response frequently determine how the public will perceive everything that follows. In the best cases, the public sees you as trustworthy and reliable. In others, your message is drowned out in the noise and confusion.

Within the first minutes and hours of an emergency, lives are on the line and so is your credibility. A PIO must balance accuracy and speed. Step into action with a clear sense of your role and how you are going to get the job done. A suboptimal initial response makes people turn elsewhere for answers. And, the first "expert" tends to be the most quoted, even if that expert is not an actual authority.

In corporate communications, United Airlines learned this lesson the hard way. The backlash to the "leggings" incident in March 2017 swirled into a full-blown crisis because the initial reply to an otherwise routine customer service inquiry via Twitter failed to recognize that the query came from someone with enormous influence. The airline's response to a question about whether it had a dress code for travelers made headlines nationwide. By the time senior executives got involved, the clumsy initial responses by a well-intentioned social media person on everyday duty shaped the story and solidified misunderstandings that the airline may never fully dispel, no matter what really happened.

When the governors of New York and New Jersey contradicted their own messages during the Ebola crisis of 2014, they not only damaged their credibility, but the confusion complicated the work necessary to keep people safe from the infectious disease. The governors both had the command of the audience in the days ahead, but their credibility as spokespeople for public health was crippled.

As Hurricane Harvey bore down on Texas in August 2017, some residents were told by state officials to evacuate while local authorities directed them to stay in place. When millions of people are in the path of a deadly storm, confusion can cost lives. And, during the storm recovery, people are less likely to heed direction from officials whose advice turned out to be wrong—no matter what the reason. People who are hurt won't care if there was a good explanation for the muddled messages.

In Sonoma County, officials have been roundly criticized for their decision not to send a countywide emergency alert when 70 mph winds pushed a record-breaking firestorm into the city of Santa Rosa late at night on Oct. 8, 2017. We will never know if any of the 44 people who died in the Northern California fires might have survived if that wireless alert had gone out, but we do know that emergency messages sent via telephone landlines failed because those lines were knocked down or burned and messages sent on the opt-in Nixle system reached only a small fraction of people in the risk areas.

In each of these situations, decisions made during the Communications Golden Hour foreshadowed the ultimate results. In emergencies, decisions must be made fast, but speed should not undermine accuracy and care. People need to see you as honest, clear, and responsive. One clumsy statement can mean that people stop listening to you, get confused, or worse.

As the World Health Organization's disease outbreak communications guidelines note, the absence of information in the earliest stages of an emergency increases the risk of rumors and inaccuracies.

> *"The parameters of trust are established in the outbreak's first official announcement. This message's timing, candor and comprehensiveness may make it the most important of all outbreak communications."*

Think about emergency communications the same way that a trauma system approaches a bleeding patient or a mass casualty incident. PIOs can benefit from the same systematic approach:

Organizing communications activities to optimize the Communications Golden Hour gets your resources into place and streamlines decisions. It lets you break from the traditional practice of detailed, inflexible plans so you can instead focus on tasks that must happen, regardless of the specific kind of crisis you are handling.

The major elements of a modern trauma system are:

- Centralized dispatchers trained to prioritize resources and give instructions

- First responders trained to standardized protocols so that they can work seamlessly even with others they never met before
- Coordinated inter-hospital transport system
- Fully equipped and staffed centralized trauma hospital able to handle emergencies anytime
- Post-surgery resources such as ICU, rehabilitation, home, and other follow-up care
- Injury research and prevention
- Post-incident evaluation and training

The analogous "emergency communications system" might look something like this:

- Clearly identified authority responsible for designating a "communications emergency"
- Public information officers trained to standardized protocols
- Pre-planned work sites, news conference locations, etc., including back-up sites
- Staffing plan that includes both initial response team and post-event "recovery" mode
- Post-incident evaluation, periodic reviews of procedures, and regular training

Each of these is *equally* critical to the ultimate outcome, which is successful dissemination of information that helps people stay safe in a dangerous situation. And that's what the Communications Golden Hour is all about.

STEPS TO MASTERING THE COMMUNICATIONS GOLDEN HOUR

Keeping the Communications Golden Hour top-of-mind as you plan, practice, and implement your emergency communications plans is the best way for your organization to be ready for any emergency of any duration.

1. **Organize your response**

   To organize response to maximize the Communication Golden Hour, you need to first identify actions needed in every emergency, then determine how large a response is needed. From there, you and your team can focus on the minute-by-minute tasks and responsibilities of the Communications Golden Hour.

   Every communications emergency requires these functions:

   - A communications person in charge.
   - A public information officer to communicate to the media and the public.
   - Somebody keeping track of who's doing what and when.
   - Designated monitoring of the news media or social media and inbound inquiries.

   In many instances, one person can handle more than one of these tasks. And, in large incidents, multiple people may be needed for each function.

2. **Determine the scale of the emergency**

   The categories of an emergency will depend on each organization. For most situations, three categories are sufficient:

   A: "All hands on deck"—a major emergency, something like Hurricane Katrina or an incident with confirmed mass casualties. It could also be a catastrophic earthquake, a raging wildfire, or anything else that is going to completely interrupt the ordinary course of business for an extended period. This is the situation where you essentially tell everybody to drop whatever else they are working on, because you need them to jump onto whatever the emergency is.

B: An incident or situation critical enough that everybody in your communications team as well as your organization needs to be aware of it, because it could get worse and might interrupt other business. Only some members of your team need to be directly involved. You will know which members of your team based on your communications protocol.

C: A limited emergency is one that interrupts the normal flow of business, but only requires a response of a few key people, such as specialists in specific areas. The emergency designation serves to alert the rest of your organization in case the situation gets bigger or if there are public or media inquiries that come in from outside your usual area. However, most normal business continues.

3. Scale your response

Use the fire service approach to scale your response:

When someone calls 911 to report a fire, a dispatcher rapidly determines how much equipment needs to roll. Food burning on someone's stove may require just one engine and a truck, but flames visible from a high rise senior housing building could trigger a citywide dispatch. Once on the scene, command staff increase or reduce the response based on what they find.

You can take the same approach to a communications emergency. The goal is to have sufficient resources in place within the critical first hour.

If the initial alert indicates an active shooter, you know you need a major level of communications. Other situations may need just a single communicator, or a response level in between.

THE COMMUNICATIONS GOLDEN HOUR: MINUTE BY MINUTE

:00-:05 Emergency begins.

- Watch commander, duty officer, or equivalent initiates response.
- If immediate danger to public, this individual should send first alert to the public via Twitter or other widely accessible channels, per protocol or plan.
- Designated communicator or PIO notified.
- Initial message should be clear, brief and direct:
  - Who is affected or in danger?
  - What should those people do?
  - Why?

Example messages:

"Emergency Alert: Suspicious package. Residents on W 27th b/t 6th and 7th Ave stay away from windows."

"Hard closure at Orange Show Rd /Waterman and Park Center Circle in San Bernardino. AVOID THE AREA - POLICE ACTIVITY!"

"NOTICE: The levee at Columbia Lakes has been breached!! GET OUT NOW!!"

"All SB lanes of I-5 blocked near Mounts Rd in Pierce County due to derailed train car. Avoid area!"

"Emergency! Armed man reported in [location]. If you are in the immediate area, go into nearest room and lock door. Await police instruction."

"Fire Dept responding to report of smoke on 6th Fl of [location]. Exit building via emergency exits now. Keep away from the area."

"Emergency! Gas leak reported at [location]. Put out any flames. Follow instructions from authorities and keep area clear for fire and utility crew access."

:05-:10 Emergency response underway.

- Incident Command established.
- PIO confirms that initial public alert has been sent and was accurate.
- PIO assesses level of communications response needed and alerts others, per plan.

:10-:15 Communications team establishes communications command post.

- Monitor social media, other sources
- Receive, track inbound media, public inquiries
- Establish media staging area, if appropriate

:15-:20 Public update.

- PIO crafts update message(s) in consultation and with approval of incident commander.
- Updated message(s) distributed via social media or other channels.
- Communications team confirms that message gets out and people respond as intended.
- These messages should confirm or supersede initial alert and provide added details, including anticipated duration of the emergency. For uncontrolled situations, give an idea of when the next update will be.

Example messages:

"PRELIMINARY INFO – Derailed Amtrak passenger train was heading south bound. Injuries and casualties reported, numbers to come. Media staging area at Eagles Pride Golf Course. #PCSD PIO Troyer en route, will not answer his cell while driving priority."

"The fire from Porter Creek road has spread very quickly and has moved down Mark West Rd to Riebli, Thomas Lake Harris towards Fountaingrove. The fire has also spread to Shiloh Ridge. Mass evacuations are taking place. If in this area, you need to move out. 911 systems are inundated. Please call only if you have an immediate emergency."

"PD investigating security threat at [location]. Please keep away until further notice."

"Update: FD investigating gas leak at [location]. [Address or name of building(s)] being evacuated. Extinguish any flames, do not light any matches, and no smoking. Keep away from area."

"All clear: Fire department has determined there is no gas leak at [location]. Normal operations and activity safe to resume."

:20-:30   Implement plan.

- Advise media of briefing schedule or other means for updates.
- Remind public that situation is fluid and details may change, if warranted.
- Request that people not share unverified information, direct them to authoritative source.

"Officer assisting a tactical team was shot by assailant. Transported to Northwestern Hospital. Updates to follow."

"MEDIA: PIO will be at the media staging area at [location]. We expect to hold a briefing at [time]."

"Please do not livestream or share tactical positions of our officers. This may put emergency responders in danger."

"Media, please refrain from live broadcasting officer positions."

"Please use common sense and restraint in circulating pics and videos of incidents at #LondonBridge and #BoroughMarket."

"In case you did not get an alert on your cell phone, authorities have issued an Emergency Alert advising of strong winds overnight creating extreme fire danger."

:30-:40 Expand communications team, if warranted.

- Communicator in charge briefs team, schedules periodic updates at fixed times.
- Ensure that relevant information from external sources is relayed to incident command promptly.
- Prepare updated media advisories based on situation and incident command direction.

Example messages:

"#BSO is working a developing incident regarding a report of active shooter located at 5901 Pine Island Rd, Parkland. Here's what we know so far: deputies are responding to reports of a shooting at Stoneman Douglas High. There are reports of victims. PIO will be on scene 3:15 PM."

"The incident at #Vauxhall is a stabbing and not connected to the incidents at #LondonBridge and #BoroughMarket."

"Media briefing expected around 4 PM at Northwestern Hospital."

:40-:45 Update to the public.

- In a major emergency, updates should be given at least every 30 minutes, even if only to let people know that there is no new information.
- Give people information on where to get more information.
- Let people know how they can help (anonymous tip line, Red Cross, etc.).

Example messages:

"All official information about the incident at [location] will be communicated on this Twitter feed."

"We are confirming that we have lost one of our own. Our officer is deceased. We are not identifying him at this time. We ask for your prayers during this tragedy. Thank you."

"We did a traffic stop of a vehicle of interest in the investigation. No one has been charged with any crime. The investigation is continuing."

:50-:55 Incident command update

- Communicator in charge confers with incident command/command staff.
- Determine who will go in front of media/public for live briefing and prepare for it.
- Schedule updates for internal stakeholders and separate updates for the public.

To organize response to maximize the Communication Golden Hour:

- Identify actions needed in every emergency
- Determine how large a response is needed for the likely scenarios
- Organize and plan around the minute-by-minute tasks and responsibilities of the Communications Golden Hour.

Chapter 3

PLAN, PRACTICE, REVISE . . . AND TWEET

"Plans are of little importance, but planning is essential."
—*Winston Churchill*

Without a communications plan, you could find yourself with no communicators showing up at the command post when they are needed. This happens too frequently—and usually means someone gets taken off other duties to be the PIO in a pinch. That person may be needed to help evacuate a building or perform other urgent operational tasks.

These are the times when essential steps are most likely missed and sometimes not even recognized until it is too late to correct. Taking too long to disseminate an evacuation message can cost lives.

The whole idea of having a communications plan in place is so that when something really bad happens, your team knows what to do. They won't waste time trying to figure out how to access the city's emergency alert system or who has the Twitter password. Instead, they can focus on the specifics of the emergency they face.

While you cannot write a plan for every contingency, you should consider the most probable ones. Fire departments pre-plan and train for "target hazards"—buildings or other places where a fire or other emergency could have a major impact. Police departments train for active shooters, terrorism, and other critical incidents. Health departments prepare for outbreaks and weather emergencies. Schools practice for evacuations and other emergency responses.

As you walk through your responses to each of these possible emergencies, consider who needs to know what is happening and how you are going to get the information to them. Twitter or Facebook may be your main channels for routine communications, but what will work best in a life-threatening emergency?

Towns throughout the Midwest and South have sirens to warn of tornadoes. Sirens are also in coastal communities of California in case of a tsunami. Many universities now automatically register incoming students, faculty, and staff into text-alert systems instead of relying on voluntary sign-ups. An increasing number of communities have opt-in systems like Nixle. Some rely on simple email distribution lists. These are all details to consider when making communications plans.

For any system to work, each part must be well-designed and -maintained and operated by trained people. Experienced communicators can work even with limited resources. Without experience and training, no software or other tools can prevent or solve problems.

Whether functioning as public information officers or in ancillary roles, communicators who respond to an emergency need to know what they are expected to do and how to do it. In addition to primary responders, other team members who may be called when extra help is needed should have the same training. Every person who might serve as an emergency communicator should be given a chance to experience their role.

A good communications plan does not have to be granular. With each sentence that you write, ask whether it is a detail that applies to every emergency. If not, then it likely can be left out. Keep documentation focused on what is most important, then trust your team to use their good judgment.

Anticipate everything that is *predictable* and *common* to all emergencies and document the desired or necessary actions ahead of time.

Plans also should include instructions on how to get the job done. This includes knowing how to activate warning systems or distribute messages via social media or any other systems. During an emergency is not the time to figure out what length messages can be distributed via your systems.

Are there web pages that need to be updated? Can your emergency message include links to those pages or attachments? These answers do not change from one type of emergency to another, so make it part of your plan for every emergency. And just because tweets now can be 280 characters long, it does not mean that long messages are helpful.

A well-crafted protocol also distinguishes between mandatory and discretionary actions. It anticipates when you expect the people in charge to do *only* what the rules say and when you expect them to exercise their own judgment based on experience and the facts specific to a situation.

The more you can simplify what happens during the Communications Golden Hour—the critical initial period—the easier everything else will be. You want your commander to focus on what is unique to the emergency at hand. At the same time, you want anyone who must be in this role to benefit from the experience of others and the effort that goes into ongoing planning and evaluation.

After the Boston Marathon bombing, hospital communicators realized that they should have closely followed existing plans for multiple casualty incidents. Although there was no plan for a bombing at the marathon and the many complications of that incident, the structure for communications already existed. Train your team that protocols are simply the bones that support their own experience and skill.

CRAFT YOUR COMMUNICATIONS EMERGENCY PLAN

Determining your communications activities in emergencies starts by answering the following questions:

What is an emergency in your organization? What is your organization's role when an emergency occurs?

Begin by identifying your department and organization's responsibilities during an emergency. Once you do so, then identify in advance how other emergency responders might be able to help. There are many emergencies where the media spokesperson for the incident command is from a different agency altogether. Know all your resources and how you might be able to use them. What other agencies or organizations are likely to be involved in an emergency response? Do they have communicators?

Who must your agency communicate with in an emergency?

Clearly identify and define your audience. In most cases, public agencies are responsible to both the public and to other public officials. However, it is unlikely that your agency is responsible for notifying the entire population of the United States or every government official at every level of government. Narrow down your audience to the people who depend on you by asking yourself the following:

- What are the demographics of your audience?
- What languages are read or spoken?
- What sources of news do they follow?
- What is their relationship with your organization?
- Do they trust you?
- Are there any special-needs or high-risk groups?
- What else could impact your ability to get urgent messages to the people you need to reach?

Who has the authority to decide when an emergency is happening?

If there is an activation of your organization's emergency operations plan, then the need for communications to respond may be obvious. However, there are situations that could be characterized as "communications emergencies" that may not involve other units of your emergency management team. Decide in advance who has the authority to make this call and how that decision is to be conveyed to the rest of the organization or the people who need to know. In some situations, this is a legal question based on statute or regulations.

Who has authority over communications when a communications emergency is declared?

Just as there can be no ambiguity about who is incident commander, there can be no ambiguity about who is the *communications* commander. In most organizations, there should be a primary, secondary, and back-up person trained and ready to take this role.

Perhaps the single most important decision that the communications commander must make is the initial determination of the scale of the emergency. Is the situation one that warrants every available person to respond, or is it a limited one that only needs one or two people?

Who gets alerted and who must show up when an emergency occurs?

This is where you think about your primary communicators and others in your organization or affiliated agencies and decide who potentially has a role in a communications emergency response. Always have a backup or two and remember that many emergencies last far longer than a single watch.

Pre-plan how these individuals will be notified and what they are expected to do. In some instances, the standard operating procedure may be to show up at their offices. In others, it may be to join a designated conference call line for instructions. In others, it may simply be, "standby until we need you." Get that all written down in your plan with corresponding contact information. Be sure to consider how frequently the internal team needs to get updates.

One more important point: Instead of designating specific people by name for each role, designate the role by title. Otherwise, your protocol becomes instantly outdated when a person changes jobs. The document needs to remain functional, no matter who the personnel are and no matter what the specific emergency is.

What happens to normal work when a communications emergency occurs?

In aviation, the concept of a "sterile cockpit" was introduced in 1981 after crash investigators determined that pilots of crashed planes may have been distracted by chatter about politics or other activities at times when they needed to be focused on landing their plane safely.

In communications, the equivalent of sterile cockpit is separating public information officers on emergency duty from their ordinary tasks. If the definition of an emergency is anything that interrupts normal business and has the potential of causing harm to people or property, you need the people handling the emergency to be laser-focused on the emergency. Let other staff handle everything else, make sure that your team knows that ordinary work can and *must* wait.

What are the communications emergency protocols?

Promulgating communications emergency protocols is an important but frequently overlooked step. These protocols need to be shared beyond your core teams. Anyone who may be called upon to respond as a communicator in an emergency must understand their role—and know that protocols exist.

When a man infected with Ebola walked into a Dallas hospital in 2014, few staff members even knew the hospital had Ebola protocols. That contributed to widespread panic, two members of the medical staff becoming infected, and many other preventable consequences far beyond that one hospital emergency department.

Other members of your emergency management team also need to understand that there is a communications protocol that designates who does what and when. Communicators need to know the extent and the boundaries of their responsibilities, and other emergency personnel need to know where duties potentially overlap, connect, or potentially conflict.

Who else might be involved in a communications emergency response?

Workshop your draft plan with the communicators or others who would be involved in an emergency response. Their feedback and buy-in to the plan is an essential factor. You need the team to understand the plan, how it works, why it exists, and—most importantly—how it affects them.

Once finalized, conduct a desktop drill with a relatively benign scenario. Desktop drills need not take more than about 90 minutes to simulate the inception of an emergency and the initial communications response. Then evaluate what happened and change anything that can be improved.

What resources are needed and available?

Once you have clarity on all the above questions, then you can address the logistics and policy aspects that come into play and identify what tools or other resources are needed.

REVIEW YOUR COMMUNICATIONS PLAN

Once you have crafted your basic plan, check to make sure it is as brief as possible. Ideally, the essential elements should fit on a wallet card that you can distribute to your team and keep in each go bag. The protocol ought to be less than three pages. Supplemental references can be much longer, of course, but basic direction must be succinct.

Review the plan with the entire team. Each person needs to know what role they perform in an emergency. The document should be by function, not name, but your team needs to know who is expected to perform in each role. Have your team run through scenarios to make sure the plan works and everyone understands it. And then revise as necessary.

PRACTICE YOUR COMMUNICATIONS PLAN

After finalizing the protocol, schedule recurring practice drills. Bring in other units of the emergency management team so that people get to know each other. Tabletop drills usually are sufficient and effective. In addition to helping people get comfortable with acting during crises, these sessions help identify ways to improve the procedures. Schedule formal practice at least quarterly.

The goal is to make sure that if an internal message goes out saying, "Category A Response: IC activated, Room 303. Briefing at 2230," everyone who gets the message knows exactly what it means for them—and then they do it. Incomplete or confusing messages are too easily ignored.

Plans only work if people are familiar with them.

Quarterly drills work well for most organizations. Busier agencies may prefer monthly or bimonthly. Fewer than quarterly pushes emergency readiness down the list of each person's priorities, so not a good idea.

After every drill, solicit feedback, then review and revise the plan, if indicated.

DO A "HOT WASH"

Equally important is a "hot wash" or review after real incidents. Recognize staff who performed well, understand where actions could have been better, and revise the plan, if there is reason. Make people comfortable sharing constructive criticism. Encourage people who recognize they need to work on their skills or knowledge.

If your communicators understand their roles and your advance planning has established work sites and other logistics, then your team can maximize efficiency—and most importantly, improve the likelihood of successful communications, even under intense pressure.

DESIGNATE SKILLED SOCIAL MEDIA COMMUNICATORS

There used to be a pause between the end of the 11 o'clock news and the next broadcasts early in the morning. Even USA Today, which revolutionized newspaper publishing with its technology and dramatically reduced the time between a reporter filing a story and the papers getting onto newsstands, used to have hours between editions. That gave PIOs some breathing room and time to pull together well-organized briefings.

Now, news gets published immediately on Twitter and other social networks, often as rough drafts are being updated as new facts emerge. There is no time between editions or newscasts. This helps if you need to get people out of harm's way fast. But, it also amplifies false or inaccurate information, especially when official sources are slow to communicate.

USE TWITTER AND OTHER SOCIAL MEDIA STRATEGICALLY

Numerous emergency agencies have adapted, many of them brilliantly. In the best examples, local news outlets trust official tweets enough to simply retweet their urgent posts before creating their own stories and members of the public turn to an agency's Facebook page for live video feeds.

"Even a mid-sized department of 50 or so officers needs to have at least one person involved in the process who understands (Twitter and other social media) and can help navigate those online outlets. If you don't, the job will be done for you. And you won't like the results," says retired police chief Joel Shults, who operates Street Smart Training.

Twitter's role in emergencies

1. Nearly 150,000 tweets went out before the first official information was provided by either of the police departments involved in the 2014 shooting of Michael Brown by a Ferguson, Missouri police officer.

2. The Dallas Police Department used Twitter effectively in the early hours of June 13, 2015, when a gunman opened fire on police headquarters. Within 30 minutes of the initial incident, the public was alerted of the gunfire. Later, when the suspect was cornered in an armored vehicle, @DallasPD sent a tweet to warn that there would be several loud shots from a large gun to shoot out the suspect vehicle windows.

3. Within 20 minutes of the mass shooting at the Inland Regional Center (IRC) in San Bernadino on Dec. 2, 2015, PIOs from the neighboring sheriff's department jumped in to help the San Bernadino Police Department. Among the first actions was tweeting out for people to stay clear of the active crime scene and where media should stage. Although San Bernadino PD had no designated PIO on duty, the sheriff's department was prepared and had practiced for major incidents like this.

4. The New York City Police Department had a few missteps when it first tried using social media, but under the leadership of then-Commissioner Bill Bratton, it evaluated its mistakes and kept moving forward. Today, NYPD sets the standard for how to use social media both for community relations and as an essential and productive tool in critical emergencies. Its worth as an emergency communications tool was proven during the 2016 Chelsea bombing and the October 31, 2017, truck attack in Lower Manhattan.

"We had to get out what we knew and what actions we needed people to take, even when we didn't know a lot," says J. Peter Donald, NYPD's assistant commissioner for communication and public information.

REMEMBER TO USE MULTIPLE CHANNELS

It also was important to push messages out via multiple channels—such as Twitter, Facebook, Instagram, and the city's voluntary NYC Alert system, in addition to the news media. That kind of targeted message cannot get out quickly unless you have people who know how their platforms work.

DON'T RELY ON OPT-IN MESSAGING

When Santa Clara County emergency officials used a system that only notified residents who voluntarily signed up for alerts, their message about imminent flooding in February 2017 reached only a few thousand people—about two-thirds of the 14,000 residents in the risk area—and there was no way to know how many people were in the area but not reached at all.

By comparison, emergency officials about 200 miles northeast used the Integrated Public Alert & Warning System (IPAWS) to warn people that damage to the Oroville Dam spillway put a wide swath of communities in jeopardy. Their Wireless Emergency Alert (WEA) message went out the same way as Amber Alerts, triggering warning sounds on mobile phones in a specified geography. IPAWS also can send messages to television and radio stations or to weather radio as well as to the WEA system. Some say these alerts are extreme, but this system is designed specifically for and restricted to use when you need people to do something quick, such as evacuate due to imminent flooding. Under FEMA rules, each state designates how these alerts are managed or triggered.

CHOOSE THE RIGHT COMMUNICATIONS METHOD

You must be careful about proofreading, but there is also nuance and interpretation to factor in. There's also ineffectiveness. We have seen in the most recent couple of years a few examples where there have been blatant communications failures because the mode of communications was poorly thought out.

An urgent message distributed on paper does nothing if the people receiving it don't pick it up and read it. Phone calls fail if the phone lines are down. Computer alerts only work if people have Internet access and devices that are online.

Communications planning means really thinking through what actions the people you're trying to get the message to must take. Unless you are clear about the goal and purpose of the communication, you are going to fail.

The following guidelines will help you begin the process to craft a solid communications plan that works – in emergencies or anytime.

GUIDELINES FOR CRAFTING YOUR PLAN

ANSWER THREE QUESTIONS

Crafting a communications emergency plan starts by answering these questions:

- **What constitutes an emergency in your organization?**

- **Who has the authority to declare a communications emergency?**

- **When an emergency is declared, who are the communicators who need to be involved?**

DESIGNATE YOUR TEAM

Create a document that includes the following groups of individuals. Be sure to note the date that it was created and keep it updated, including the date of last review on the document. This roster should be updated at least annually and anytime there are personnel changes.

- Identify the specific people with the authority to declare a "communications emergency."
- Identify the specific people expected to show up in any emergency. (These are the people who are needed no matter what the scope of the crisis may be.)
- Identify the specific people expected to be the back-ups to the people expected to show up in any emergency.
- Identify the people who are expected to show up for specific types of emergencies or for specific duties that may be needed. For example, this could be task-based, such as social media or administrative support. Or, it could be sectors of your organization, such as infectious disease, natural disaster, or bioterrorism.
- Identify all the other personnel who could be tapped for communications responsibilities in an emergency.

DEFINE RESPONSE/DISPATCH LEVELS

Define three levels of emergencies, based on the resources needed for each. For each category, specify:

- who needs to respond,
- where they need to report, and
- what the priorities are.

A: "All hands"

B: Key personnel respond; others standby for further instructions.

C: Limited response.

Chapter 4

DEVELOP THE RIGHT MESSENGERS

To be persuasive we must be believable; to be believable we must be credible; to be credible we must be truthful.

—Edward R. Murrow

Effective emergency communications means getting a precisely crafted and actionable message to the intended audience rapidly. You need the right words, at the right time, by the right messenger.

The right words are clear, direct, and actionable, with authority and facts to back them up. They are the opposite of ambiguity.

If the public needs to take action for their own or others' safety, the right time is the earliest moment when the accuracy and urgency of the message is established.

Use the mnemonic CASE: The right messenger for emergency information must be credible, accurate, succinct, and empathetic.

And the right *messengers* are needed to amplify your message outside of your organization. Bravado may help first responders get through difficult incidents, but the ability to relate to the audience is more important when communicating about a situation when lives are on the line.

Once spokespersons are selected, be clear on what you are trying to accomplish, whose behavior you are trying to influence, and why. If you want to effectively get people out of the way of danger or simply change what they are doing, you must understand their interests and the messenger they will trust.

CHOOSING YOUR MESSENGERS

Every emergency organization needs a skilled public information officer and one or more executives who can effectively brief the public under the glare of TV lights. However, getting urgent information to the public requires much more. In stressful emergencies, especially mass casualty incidents, major crimes, or natural disasters, having people outside your organization to echo your messages can provide both reassurance and solid information to your constituents.

Taking a "surround-sound" to communications increases success and builds good will, an essential element if something ever goes wrong. Also, in long-duration emergencies, your agency may need extra help from community members.

In the era of social media superstars and influencers who come and go by the hour, choosing the right messenger can be perplexing and complicated. There is no formula for instant or guaranteed success, but the steps that follow will increase your chances of selecting the right person for the right message.

At the same time, familiarizing everyone with the principles of public communication is also important. All public employees—at least those who are in supervisory roles—must know how to communicate, even if that is not part of their primary job. Public health professionals learn how to communicate in a crisis when they are in graduate school, because it is an important element of a public health degree. Some police and fire departments provide public information training to command officers, but many do not. In these days of ubiquitous social media especially, any firefighter, any cop, any government employee can very quickly become the face of their agency. Even a little training can help.

Start with your own people

Here are factors to consider when selecting the right messenger for the job:

- Rank: In major incidents, the person in charge may be the most appropriate. Every police or fire chief, emergency management leader, city manager, or mayor needs to be ready for this. However, every agency should have at least one and ideally two alternate speakers. These individuals should have sufficient rank to have credibility, but they do not necessarily need to be command staff. Access to the facts and ability to communicate are the most important factors. Rank is secondary.

- Reputation: Individuals who already have a community's trust have an instant advantage over others. If trust is already established, your messages are much more likely to work. Know when an unknown spokesperson may be beneficial. Try to avoid individuals associated with controversy—but only if there are other legitimate authorities. Use a known spokesperson to introduce other authorities if they are unknown or lesser known.

- Responsiveness: An effective public information officer must be accessible and responsive to public and media requests. This does not necessarily mean answering cell phones between scheduled briefings, but the PIO must be actively engaged in the public communications operation while the head of a department presumably is focused on incident command.

- Rehearse: No matter how many live briefings a spokesperson has given, there is always something to learn from exercising those skills. Set up and rehearse practice media briefings that give your secondary spokespeople a chance to experience being in the spotlight.

Connect with a network of credible leaders to amplify your messages

Here are some things to consider when working with those outside of your organization:

- Trust: Who are the people that your community members respect? Start with civic leaders, elected officials, and others already in the public eye. Then look to smaller geographic or social groups where religious leaders, activists, and small business people may be able to help.

- Interact: Establish your network of amplifiers before the next emergency so that they know what to expect and what to do. Engage these people regularly so that you get feedback from the community. This works best if they hear from you routinely, not just when there is an emergency.

- Build: You need multiple people to amplify your message, especially when there are language, cultural, or other differences within your community. Rarely does one person cover all the bases. Some groups may look to a celebrity, others to their pastor, and still others to an elected official. Use people outside of official roles as connectors to groups that you may not have direct access to on a regular basis.

Make sure your messenger speaks the right language

In addition to language, look at the factors that influence people. Who does your audience listen to and why? In some places, there may be a television anchor or other personality with significant influence. In ethnic groups, there may be a media or arts celebrity known mostly to people who speak a language other than English. Sometimes, one part of a community respects the same person who is rejected by others across town. The more you understand this, the more likely you are to find ways to channel urgent messages to everyone.

This also is where dialect comes in. A spokesperson will have more credibility if they speak in the familiar dialect. Dominican-Americans use different words from Mexican-Americans or Puerto Ricans, just as phrases commonly used by English-speaking Americans from places like Alabama and Arkansas differ from common phrases in the Northeast. These differences are far more nuanced than simply what word do we use to refer to sugary drinks or sandwiches on long rolls.

Rely on community allies

Community allies are important when emergencies continue for a long time, such as health emergencies. Especially if resources are stretched and residents feel as if they have not heard from government, a community ally who says she has heard directly from an official can do a lot to allay concerns.

Community relationships also change, just as populations and neighborhoods do. Periodically checking to see whether there is a new community of immigrants with their own language should be part of any comprehensive emergency plan review and another messenger chosen.

Over time, one of the things that has proven absolutely consistent is that people are most receptive to messages when they hear them from somebody who is most like them, with language being the most straightforward credential. One health campaign I worked on many years ago was a dismal failure because the sponsor would only permit communications in English and Spanish. That was not a good way to establish credibility with a target audience that primarily spoke Tagalog or Vietnamese. These people already felt marginalized, so a health campaign that disregarded their language made this worse, not better—even for the members of the community who understood either of the languages used in the campaign.

Before the next emergency, give your designated spokespersons opportunities to establish themselves with media and the community. The more comfortable they are with being in the public spotlight, the easier the next emergency will be. And, your team can focus on crafting the right messages without needing to worry that the spokesperson has never been on live TV.

The right messenger with the right message:

—Has access to facts

—Speaks clearly in widely understood language

—Connects with community between incidents

GOING LIVE

Going in front of the media is perhaps the most important and riskiest part of emergency communications. Ideally you have public information officers who are experienced with doing interviews, especially on live television. An emergency is not the time for somebody to have their first on-camera experience.

Most police and other public officials have gotten accustomed to the idea that cameras now are everywhere, and you must presume that what you are saying is being transmitted live on the Internet—and can never be erased. This means being ready to speak intelligently and professionally, sometimes without more than a few minutes to get ready.

It is not uncommon for media to surround a police car when a senior official or a public information officer arrives on the scene, expecting a news conference the minute the car door opens. You cannot control that, but you can anticipate that this will happen so that you are able to maintain composure.

Also, prepare an appropriate way to end questions on the spot, for example: "I know you are eager to get details. As you can see I've just arrived. Give me a few minutes, and I will share what I can with you."

Use your chosen spokesperson

The optimal structure of a media briefing in an emergency is to have one spokesperson with a message that includes all the key details. The spokesperson should step up to the media staging area, wait until the cameras and journalists are ready, then begin by introducing themselves and giving a brief, succinct statement. The words need to be chosen carefully. The statement should be given slowly. The spokesperson needs to convey an appropriate level of concern.

Stay on message

Before a spokesperson begins any interaction with the media in an emergency, make sure that he or she is clear on the purpose. What is the Single Overriding Communications Objective (SOCO) for this incident? What do people need to know, and what do they need to do? If there is an immediate danger to the public, focus on that message. Do not dilute the key message with miscellany.

Pay attention to staging

Be mindful of what is in the background. Having an emergency vehicle as the backdrop helps control what is behind the messenger and prevents distractions, such as people walking around. This is not always possible. Consider how many uniformed personnel should be in the picture. Make sure there is nothing in the immediate location that is sensitive for any reason. This includes anything that might be offensive, gruesome, or otherwise distracting from the message.

Dress for work

The spokesperson should wear whatever they would normally wear on the job. If it is a police chief, then a uniform is appropriate. If it is a physician who is treating patients, then a white coat fits. However, the uniform must be authentic. A hospital administrator who is not seeing patients has no reason to wear a white coat. And a police chief would not show up at a crime scene wearing a dress uniform. The uniform should be clean and professional, but it should be the real thing, not a prop. In a natural disaster, nobody expects emergency responders to have spotless uniforms or shiny new protective gear.

State obvious facts

If the coroner was seen taking a body away, acknowledge that there was a fatality. If flames are visible, say there is a fire. If there is a visible logo of a major company on a vehicle involved in the crash, mention it if it helps people understand the incident. The spokesperson can say "the truck with the [company name] logo on it" without assigning blame or jumping to any conclusions.

When in doubt, leave it out

Uncertain details are not facts. It is always better to say "we do not have the exact number yet" instead of giving a number likely to change.

Convey the scale of the incident

The media and others focus on numbers. Emergency responders focus on people and their families. Giving out numbers that turn out to be wrong ends up hurting more than helping. Convey the scale of an incident, but save the precision for later. Once the carnage in Las

Vegas was determined to involve "dozens" of casualties, the public knew that this was a major incident. The exact number was not important to include in public information during the response. If the number is likely to change significantly, give yourself wiggle room with phrasing like, "We have at least a dozen victims" instead of "We have 12 victims."

Chapter 5

CRAFT THE RIGHT MESSAGE

"I love the right words. Economy and precision of language are important."
—Chelsea Clinton

The ability to do precision wordsmithing under pressure is one of the most important and difficult skills for any emergency communicator. There is a delicate balance between "enough" and "too much" information when you need people to act fast. This is even more challenging when health or safety risks are involved and people need to make quick decisions for their own or their loved ones' well-being.

When writing any urgent or emergency message, put yourself in the shoes of the people receiving it. Give enough detail for the audience to take the actions that you need them to take. Clearly state the threat, who and what is at risk, and what to do.

In an emergency, you communicate urgent messages because you need people to do something: evacuate, shelter-in-place, be alert, stay calm, or any one of dozens of possibilities. If you have planned well, figuring out the right message for your audience can start within the first minutes. Inadequate planning means precious time gets lost figuring out what message to send or even how to send it.

Urgent information is anything that people need to protect themselves. It is information that without which people could be harmed. Urgent information is something that you need to keep yourself, your employees, your families, and your communities safe.

At the same time, the pressure of an emergency is when someone might forget that the word "investigation" means one thing to police and another to health professionals, or that the word "backup" has many different possible definitions. A message intended to calm a community easily can become alarming if misinterpreted.

Tim Burrows, former Toronto police officer and one of the leading voices on law enforcement communications, found this out the hard way when he said, "Gas has been deployed." For law enforcement insiders, that just means that officers in the area have the gas available, but the public heard something different—that tear gas was being used.

Emergency messages need to be crafted with precision so that they are quickly and accurately understood. To do that, you need to be clear about what your audience needs to know and what they already know or believe.

Human behavior also comes into play. People with facts must be assertive with them while also being mindful that the audience may be reluctant to accept them. An emergency message without facts has no credibility.

Truly urgent warnings must be simple, clear and direct—without nuance:

> *"Leave your home now: Fire advancing fast to Hwy 116 & Midway Dr area. Evacuate via Montgomery Rd to Taft HS. Take only pets and essentials."*

That is far stronger than, "People in the area of Hwy 116 & Midway are advised to evacuate. Shelter set up at Taft HS. Wildfire advancing rapidly from the east."

Also important: Properly distinguish between messages that describe immediate urgent action and those that are providing less urgent information, such as about resources or others. Keeping doors locked because of a dangerous suspect at-large would be an example of an urgent message, while advisories in advance of a forecast weather hazard would be in the latter category.

If you use the Everbridge Nixle system:

- "emergency alerts" are intended for messages warranting immediate action;
- "advisories" are to provide information about crime or traffic but not necessitating immediate action; and,
- "community" messages are for such things as local news or event notices.

Categorizing messages correctly is essential: some people elect to only receive "emergency" messages. That is a problem if an emergency management agency puts evacuation notices out as "advisories" when a fast-moving wildfire advances, which has happened. Similarly, if routine or political messages are sent out as advisories or alerts, then people will opt out from the emergency notifications.

TAILOR MESSAGES TO YOUR EXACT COMMUNITY

Strong relationships and ongoing interactions with community allies give you wisdom that helps you craft the right messages for emergency and other situations. Knowing what your audience understands, knowing who they trust, and knowing what resources they have are all essential for precision wordsmithing.

Know the demographics of your audience, know who people trust, and know where they turn for news. In addition to differences based on age, differences also exist based on region, economic status, and between rural and urban geographies.

They are also relevant in any ongoing communications, of course. For example, if you are trying to reduce smoking in Arizona, your influencer for the city of Phoenix is unlikely to be an influencer in Flagstaff. If you are fighting diabetes, your messages need to be tailored to the specific community that you are targeting. Telling people to eat five servings of fruits and vegetables a day will fall on deaf ears in neighborhoods where fresh fruits and vegetables are hard to find.

In emergencies, this comes into play when you give directions such as "use air conditioning" during a heat emergency. Not everyone has air conditioning, so they may tune out if that is the first part of your message. Be sensitive to different groups and always lead your message with instructions that apply in the broadest way possible.

This is also true regarding language and dialect. Although English is the primary language in the United States, emergency communications need to be conducted in multiple languages if there are people who do not understand English. In non-urgent situations, using multiple languages shows respect to your audience. In urgent situations, this can be the difference between success and failure.

In your planning, include data that show how many people have something other than English as their primary language. Then plan ways to get your emergency messages to those people. If many people speak Spanish, consider conducting briefings in both English and Spanish. Make connections with organizations that can help deliver your messages to those who speak other languages. Know your community and what languages are spoken there.

Most commonly spoken languages in the USA:

1. English
2. Spanish
3. Chinese
4. Tagalog
5. Vietnamese
6. Arabic
7. French
8. Korean
9. Russian
10. German

Source: U.S. Census Bureau, 2016

This type of "narrowcasting" is also important for ongoing communications, and it may be especially important if you are trying to change behavior. For example, to get messages about the Zika virus to the people most at risk, specific messages needed to be developed for specific immigrant groups. The message for people from Cuba could not be identical to the messaging used for people who came to the United States from Barbados.

The health risks may have been similar, but the people receiving the messages did not identify themselves as connected. Once messages were targeted directly to people likely to travel to each of the affected countries, the outbreak became more manageable.

ELEMENTS OF AN EFFECTIVE EMERGENCY MESSAGE

Ask these questions to craft an emergency message that works:

- What is the specific hazard?
- Who is at risk?
- Where is the danger? How big is the danger?
- When did it or will it start? When will the danger be over?
- Why is this credible? Who is the source of the information?
- How can people stay safe?
- When was this message issued? And by whom?

Messages also should distinguish between what is certain (e.g., streets closed; suspects in custody; flooding happening now) and variables (e.g., risk of flooding; hurricane or tornado forecast; uncontrolled crime scene.)

While messages need to be brief, they must also be complete. If a warning message goes out without actionable information or enough detail to show its credibility, recipients are more likely to ignore it. "Research has shown that people need sufficient information to validate their risk and spur them to take appropriate action," according to the Federal Emergency Management Agency.

Also, be mindful of the tools used to disseminate your messages. Some systems automatically add headers that take up space. People who receive alerts via email may only see the subject line. Make sure that the first words are the most important ones. And, be careful to follow the character count limit that applies to your alert system. Wireless Emergency Alerts that light up cell phones are limited to 90 characters until systems are upgraded to handle 360, which is in progress. However, some cell phones will only handle the shorter messages even after systems are upgraded.

For these reasons and others, be sure to put the most important information within the first five or six words of any message—no matter how long it will be. Tweets can be 280 characters now, but sticking to the older 140-character limit makes your message easier for people to quickly grasp.

Another problem in fast-changing situations is sequence and timing. Information gets outdated rapidly, so people need to be able to look at a message and quickly determine if it is new or old. Many agencies include a sequential number for each alert. Looking at message #9 makes it easy to know that message #8 is older, even if a neighbor just forwarded it. All messages should have a time marker. If your system does not add that automatically, include it in your message. For example, "As of 9 PM, the situation has not changed. Next update will be at 11 PM."

STEP-BY-STEP GUIDE TO EMERGENCY MESSAGE CRAFTING

Evaluate: What are you trying to communicate, and why? What is the urgent action you need people to take?

For example, consider this message:

The university has received a bomb threat. Police are responding. The campus is closed until further notice. Please keep away.

Or consider this alternative:

CAMPUS CLOSED: Police responding to a security issue. Please keep away until further notice.

Both are under 140 characters, but the second one is much more likely to get the key message across. The key message is "keep away." The inclusion of "bomb threat" in the first version does two things that go against what you need: people will focus on the bomb threat and they may not even read to the part where you tell them to keep away.

Of course, you need to explain the reason for the closure at an appropriate time, which might be just a few minutes later, but that is a very different message from an urgent command to keep clear of a dangerous scene.

If you are a government agency or federally funded institution or organization, public information is part of your core responsibility. If there is something *urgent* happening in the community, you must tell people about it. And, if there's something preventable that *could* happen in the community, you should talk about it.

One important caveat: Make sure that the people you are messaging can do what you direct them to do. In New Orleans, many of the people told to evacuate had no means of transportation to evacuation centers, even if they could get out from flooded homes.

"Why would you get in the public media and ask a city where 80 percent of its citizens ride public transport to evacuate? What were they supposed to do? Fly? Get on a broom?" community leader Dyan French Cole told Congress at a hearing on the government response to Katrina.

Consider: How much detail does your audience need? What information should be protected?

Whenever experts like public safety executives, scientists, or other specialists need to craft a public message, they need to think carefully about how much detail is needed.

To figure out how much detail to include, you must put yourself in the shoes of your audience. You must use language that is relevant and unambiguous. You need to provide enough to make your message credible, but not so much that you muddle your message. Cut to the chase, then stop.

If you are communicating about an emergency at a school, your message to parents likely needs to be different from your message to the general public. Parents need to know where their children are. The public only needs to know that the children are safe.

If you want people to take extra care because of a heat wave, does it matter whether it is 103 degrees or 105? No. Keep it simple. "Record heat again today. Cooling centers are open for those who need safe shelter. And, please check on elderly neighbors."

Determine: What is most important *right now*?

Here is an example that illustrates messaging that clearly recognizes what facts the audience most urgently needs. When Amtrak train #501 derailed south of Seattle in November 2017 during morning rush hour, the first public message was a traffic advisory:

*"All SB lanes of I-5 blocked near Mounts Road in Pierce County
due to derailed train car. Avoid area!" said the tweet from the
Washington State Department of Transportation.*

While many people wanted to know details about the accident,
the *most important* public message was for people to steer clear of the
emergency scene and that the highway was blocked. In other words, if
you want to get to work, go a different way. There was nothing else about
the train accident that directly affected people more than the traffic jam.

More information came about 30 minutes later from the local law
enforcement agency:

*"PRELIMINARY INFO - Derailed Amtrak passenger train
was heading south bound. Injuries and casualties reported,
numbers to come. Media staging area at Eagles Pride Golf
Course. #PCSD PIO Troyer en route, will not answer his cell
while driving priority."*

Five minutes later, the Washington State Patrol sent this message
with logistics for media:

*"WSP on scene of train derailment across SB i-6 at Mounts Rd.
@wspd1pio will handle traffic. @Amtrak will handle media
related to incident."*

Determine: What does your audience know?

Safety during an emergency largely depends on preparedness, which
means that people need to know about risks in advance—and most
importantly, they need to know how to prepare and what to do when
a disaster occurs. Even in California, where earthquakes are part of
everyday life and lore, too many people are misinformed about how
to stay safe, and few are prepared for what to do after an earthquake.

When we asked a randomly selected sample of Californians, an alarming 15 percent said they do not know what to do when an earthquake happens. Of those who *think* they know what to do, more than 25 percent said they would either run outside or stand in a doorframe—even though experts say neither of those are good ways to stay safe.

Back when buildings were built from unreinforced brick, door frames were somewhat safer and stronger than other parts of a structure. That is not the case in most modern buildings, and finding shelter from falling debris or protecting yourself from getting knocked over is recommended instead. But the old advice sticks.

This level of misunderstanding presents an important challenge to emergency management officials. Messages must be crafted knowing that many people on the other end of your communication have incomplete or even wrong safety information.

Consider: What does your audience believe about the situation?

This is where credibility and existing relationships play a major role. If your agency has a great relationship with your community, people are inclined to pay attention to you in a crisis. However, if the audience either does not know you or has a negative attitude toward you— deserved or not—getting emergency messages across will require extra effort.

> *"Simply telling people that their views are invalid does not work,"* says Jeff Rubin, emergency manager for the Tualatin Valley Fire and Rescue District in Oregon. If people are afraid, even if based on false information, that fear is "not irrational."

Few issues illustrate this better than the perception among some people that vaccines can cause autism or other harm to children. When a community has a measles outbreak, experts must recognize that some people believe the vaccines-autism link, even if the facts show that they are wrong. It does not matter that this view is not supported by science or that its leading proponent committed scientific fraud.

In a 2013 study that tested four different types of messages to promote vaccination, researchers found that pro-vaccine messages reduce the likelihood that parents will have their children vaccinated *if* they had a negative attitude toward vaccinations *before* hearing the message.

Unconscious bias can also affect the impact of your message. "You can communicate better if you are aware of bias. Most of the time, the bias is unconscious," says Rubin. "When people get down to their basal fears, their IQ immediately drops 50 points."

However, emergency communicators cannot simply say, "Don't worry" or "You are wrong." If a person believes they can get Ebola from casual contact or simply living in the same city as someone who is sick, there is nothing irrational about wanting to get away from what that person believes is a risk.

Rubin says focus on actions that people can take to stay safe instead of trying to correct the incorrect perceptions. "Give people options, tell them how they can make themselves safer."

The point is, do not challenge the beliefs of your target audience. That gives people reason to reject your instructions at the very time that you need to be considered a trusted source of safety information.

Examine: How can you make your message unequivocal, clear, and actionable for the people you're trying to reach?

Effective messages and emergency instructions need to be clear, direct, and as simple as possible. They must also be immediately relevant. If you include extraneous information, you will lose your chance to communicate effectively. If you use uncommon words or too many words, you sacrifice clarity.

Instead of telling people to "evacuate to a safe area," which leaves too much to be interpreted, be more specific: "If you are outside, get away from buildings or other structures to avoid falling objects." That is short enough to fit in a text message or tweet, too.

Personal contact matters. When emergency responders go door-to-door to get people out of flooding danger, they get maximal response—close to 100 percent in some cases. Without that direct contact, compliance of 75 percent is hard to achieve.

Convey: What can people do?

Every public safety emergency message should include information about what people should do—even if you just want them to stay calm and do nothing. People instinctively want to help. Remember to channel their energy in the right direction.

If your message directs people to "take shelter," you need to help them find shelter.

If your message says shelter in place, you need to give an idea of when the situation might change.

If you are pursuing a dangerous suspect and just want people to stay away, include how people can report tips if they have information.

Choose: What are the right words?

When you are giving out information at the beginning of an incident, make sure that you let people know that the situation is evolving and information is preliminary. Say, "We don't have complete information. This may change."

- Promise updates and give a time frame.
- And do not minimize a situation that could escalate.

- Beware of misunderstood or ambiguous words. If you include a street name, make sure there is only one street that matches your words. Do not use jargon or abbreviations, unless universally recognized.

A few examples of words that can be easily misunderstood

- Backup—could be computer, tactical, or many other things
- Casualty—public hears "dead" when this term applies to injured or dead
- Deployed—are the officers carrying gas or using it?
- First Responder—use firefighter, police officer, etc.
- Investigate/investigation—suggests criminal situation
- Recovery—could mean retrieving a body or healing from injury
- Stable—stable can apply to any condition, including dead
- Trauma—frequently misunderstood as psychological injury, not physical
- Unconscious—suggests severity but by itself has broad meaning

Determine: What numbers are necessary?

In an emergency, giving people access to detailed information may be important, but that does not mean that every official statement should be chock-a-block with minutiae. The opposite works better.

Verbal messages should include only essential information, and, generally, only one specific number. Even written messages should avoid too much detail. Saying "one out of 10" is easier for people to grasp on-the-fly than saying "one-tenth" or "10 percent." In writing, the specific number is better, both because it is more precise and because it uses fewer characters.

Do not provide numbers that are uncertain. In a mass casualty incident, avoid providing a specific number, especially in the early hours. After the Aurora, Colorado theater shooting in 2012, police had to revise their casualty count downward. Although their overall communications on the incident was done very well, this revision could have been avoided if they had not given a specific number while the situation was unfolding.

Do not exaggerate. Be realistic. You cannot minimize a big problem.

More than anything else, you never want to put a message out that could turn out to be wrong.

Show that you care, without the scientific mumbo jumbo

Public information officers are the mediators between technical experts and the broader population. There is a natural tension between scientists and the public, and communications professionals are caught in the middle. Scientists are trained to be precise, to back up every statement with supporting evidence, and to avoid speculation. The public tends to jump to conclusions based on scant evidence, and many tune-out when supporting facts are provided.

People "don't care about how crazily advanced you are" when facing health or other major life decisions, says Mehmet Oz, better known as TV's "Dr. Oz." Oz went from being a renowned heart surgeon and university researcher to afternoon television talk show host, largely because he knows how to explain complicated health matters in plain language.

But even Dr. Oz was surprised at the gap between the public's interest in learning and how knowledge actually transfers. People in scary situations say they want facts and science, but often, they just want to hear someone they trust tell them what to do.

"People want to be comfortable that you are making the right judgment, but they don't want to be confused with some of the side messaging that doctors use when talking to each other," he says. Heart patients are more concerned about whether they will get back to a normal lifestyle and whether surgery will leave big scars than they are about the latest research data or the science behind their treatment.

"Convey what you are doing without the scientific mumbo jumbo," he says.

That principle applies to almost any field, especially in emergencies. One of the best ways to establish credibility at the start of a briefing on a dangerous situation is for the spokesperson to acknowledge how people feel. Words like, "We know that people in the community are concerned," or "We are doing everything we can to help the victims," or "This is a difficult time for the family" help connect on a human level.

Be proactive: Correct and clarify any discrepancies

Especially in emergencies, authorities may disagree. When you know that another agency is saying something different, acknowledge it. If the other agency has authority over a different aspect of the incident or its people are in a different position, those explanations will make sense to most people. If there is a genuine disagreement, you will have more credibility by addressing it straight-on instead of only giving your position and hoping reporters never find the other.

For example, there are times when U.S. health authorities may give different guidance from the World Health Organization. This happened during the initial phase of the Zika outbreak in 2016. Anyone looking at the two recommendations would be curious about the difference, so the question will come up. You might as well explain it.

If the World Health Organization says, "There's no need to avoid travel to certain countries," and the Centers for Disease Control and Prevention says, "We think you should avoid traveling to certain countries," the CDC's official message should add another sentence, such as: "Even though the World Health Organization says there is no need to avoid traveling here, we think pregnant women ought to avoid traveling here because of the risk of birth defects."

Communicate: What are the next steps after the emergency?

In communications after an emergency, let people know what happens next. If there will be a long investigation, when will updates be provided? Where will the next information come from?

Recognize the work of your agency and others who participated in the emergency response. Give an update on whether normal business or normal operations have resumed. If they have not, why not, and when will they resume?

Let people know that your agency is doing its job, but do not be afraid to acknowledge that your agency includes humans with feelings.

Some police departments have asked people to refrain from ordinary business in the immediate aftermath of a critical incident—either because so many people were involved in the incident or because people were coping with the trauma of a deadly situation or other impactful event. Well-meaning citizens frequently order food for first responders. If this is helpful, give people instructions. If it is unhelpful, thank people for the good intentions but ask them to not to.

Acknowledge tragedy. Even when a death results from an individual's criminal acts, there still are grieving family and friends. There is no downside risk to expressing sincere compassion, if you have credibility and choose words carefully.

"The department extends its condolences to the family and friends of the deceased" is one example from the Chicago Police Department.

Post-incident messages should focus on the future, including resilience, rebuilding, or repairs. They also should focus on what your agency will do to prepare for or prevent the next emergency.

When a department faces criticism, acknowledge it, and commit to supporting the appropriate after-action evaluation, independent investigation, or whatever process applies. People look to assign blame whenever bad things happen. Stay out of the fray, do not take it personally, and focus on continuing to protect the public in a professional way.

COMMUNICATING ABOUT SCIENCE AND HEALTH

During the Ebola scare of 2014, the public was not listening when scientists cited study after study showing that the deadly virus only spreads through close physical contact with an infected person. Three decades of research meant nothing to people who were already conditioned to be afraid.

Part of the problem was how the experts used the data. Instead of picking one main talking point, they unleashed a rash of information. In the news conference by the Centers for Disease Control and Prevention confirming the first Ebola case in the United States, the transcript shows a lot of big words and the absence of a single clear message.

Technical terms like "incubation period," "interventions," and "nonspecific" muddled what was intended as the key message: that a traveler from Liberia was being treated in a Texas hospital with a confirmed Ebola infection and that the isolated case was not a risk to people who had not been in close, direct contact with the patient.

Here is how CDC Director Tom Frieden opened up the briefing:

> Good afternoon, everybody. Thanks for joining us. As you have been hearing us, Ebola is a serious disease. It's only spread by direct contact with someone who's sick with the virus. It's only spread through body fluids. The incubation period is 8 to 10 days after exposure. Can be as short as two days or as long as 21 days. It's a severe disease which has a high case fatality rate, even with the best of care. But there are core tried and true public

health interventions that stop it. Today, we are providing the information that an individual traveling from Liberia has been diagnosed with Ebola in the United States. This individual left Liberia on the 19th of September, arrived in the U.S. on the 20th of September, had no symptoms when departing Liberia or entering this country, but four or five days later around the 24th of September began to develop symptoms. On the 26th of September initially sought care and Sunday the 28th of September was admitted to a hospital in Texas and placed on isolation. We received in our laboratory today specimens from the individual, tested them and they tested positive for Ebola. The state of Texas also operates a laboratory that found the same results. Testing for Ebola is highly accurate. It's a PCR test of blood. So, what does this mean? The next steps are basically threefold. First, to care for the patient. We'll be hearing from the hospital shortly, to provide the most effective care possible as safely as possible to keep to an absolute minimum the likelihood, the possibility that anyone would become infected. Second, to maximize the chances that the patient might recover. Second, we identify all people who may have had contact with the patient while he could have been infectious. Remember, Ebola does not spread from someone who is not infectious. It does not spread from someone who doesn't have fever and other symptoms. It's only someone who is sick with Ebola who can spread the disease. Once those contacts are all identified, they are all monitored for 21 days after exposure to see if they develop fever. If they develop fever then those same criteria are used to isolate them and make sure they are cared for as well as possible so they maximized their chances and to minimize or eliminate the chance that they would infect other people. The bottom line here is that I have no doubt that we will control this importation or case of Ebola so it does not spread widely in this the country.

If you dissect this opening statement from the perspective of a healthcare expert, Frieden's messages make sense. However, if the goal is to convey essential information to the public, you can also see why the main message got lost. Frieden did not do what the CDC media team has mandated for years: identify your *single overriding communication objective* (SOCO) before starting to talk. The SOCO model demands discipline that pays off when communicating to the public. What is your one message, and what are three facts to support it? Period.

Instead of the five-minute speech, Frieden's messages would have been much more clear if he had done two things differently. One, he needed to have a simple, direct message. Two, that message needed to be backed up with clear supporting points. Here is how I might have shaped his opening remarks:

> Good afternoon, everybody. Thanks for joining us. Today, we are sharing information about a person who traveled from Liberia to Dallas and now is being treated for Ebola. Ebola is a serious disease, but I want everyone to understand some facts about it. Ebola only spreads by direct contact with the bodily fluids of someone who is sick with Ebola. Only a person who has a fever or other symptoms of illness is infectious. Even then, transmission requires direct contact with that person's blood, urine, or other bodily fluids. You cannot get Ebola just by being near a person who has the disease.

Instead of five minutes, the key points are laid out directly in 45 seconds. If the news media or the public tuned out after this point, the key message would still come through. Effective communication requires understanding that few people—even reporters whose jobs require it—listen past the first minute. Get your key messages up front, simply and succinctly.

When Bob Howard led the CDC's communications office, he used SOCO as a tool to educate scientists about the difference between clear public communication and scientific precision. He used this example to illustrate this point: If you are a public health official trying to reduce foodborne illness from *E.coli* infection, instead of explaining how complex *E.coli* is or how it can be spread throughout the food chain, the main public message needs to focus.

Instead of this:

"E. coli O157:H7 is a complex pathogen whose proliferation is tied to issues as far-reaching as meat production and processing, day-care centers, cooking times, handwashing, and pasteurization."

Say this:

"Cook hamburger until well done, drink pasteurized beverages, and wash your hands well and frequently."

The same is true when communicating about diseases spread by rats, bats, or mice. Instead of going into detail about a specific virus or the science behind your public message, boil it down to, "Avoid contact with rodents."

SOCO has become so well-integrated into the CDC culture that Hollywood included it in the 2011 movie Contagion, in a scene where Kate Winslet, playing an epidemiologist, had to review her SOCO with her boss before going in front of the media about a virus that had already killed five people. In the film, the key message was boiled down to "We're isolating the sick and quarantining those who we believe were exposed."

Reflecting on how the Ebola outbreak played out, National Institute of Allergy and Infectious Diseases director Anthony Fauci noted that, "In the United States, certainly fear of Ebola spread much faster than Ebola itself."

More succinct messaging from health officials could have made a difference. Instead, overly complex messages opened the door for politicians and self-proclaimed experts to drive the public discussion— and hysteria.

Communicating about science in the Twitter era is a perplexing issue. Science communication has never been easy, but the principles remain unchanged: understand your audience and know the difference between precision and accuracy.

Always being accurate is not the same as always being precise. If you are talking about 11 percent, you can say "about one out of every 10." That is still accurate, but which is clearer? If you're speaking verbally, "about one out of every 10" is going to come across much better. This is the kind of thinking you must do as a communicator, knowing that you would never write a phrase as imprecise in a scientific paper.

The way to determine the right amount of detail is to look carefully at whether it makes a difference. Ask yourself does the person being addressed need to know that level of detail. Does that detail change the behavior of the person receiving it? Include just enough detail to prompt the action you need them to take.

"You have to say what is relevant to the people who are listening," says Linda Fried, M.D., dean of the Mailman School of Public Health at Columbia University.

"Scientists are not trained to communicate effectively with people who are not also trained as scientists," says Fried. "I have spent a lot of my career trying to bend my scientific training tendencies in order to say what actually can be meaningful to the people who are listening."

PUTTING IT ALL INTO ACTION: THE SINGLE OVERRIDING COMMUNICATION OBJECTIVE

The concept of *single overriding communication objective* (SOCO) was developed at the Centers for Disease Control and Prevention and is a useful tool to organize key messages intended to get people to act. When you know your audience, understand your resources, and have a clear sense of what needs to be communicated, this process streamlines key message development.

What is your key message?

In one sentence, what is the single main point that you want your audience to understand. Keep it simple. This is what you would like to see or hear in news coverage or social media posts.

Why is important to convey this message?

What do you want people to do after hearing your key message? In other words, why communicate about this now?

Who needs to hear this message?

Identify your target audience. Is there a geographic, demographic, or other segment that is most important to reach? In most instances, you have multiple audiences—decide who is your most important (primary) audience and your next most important (secondary.) Generally, the news media is a conduit to your audience, not a primary or secondary audience itself.

What facts support your key message?

Identify at least three convincing details that make your key message believable. Use facts that your target audience will understand, accept, and remember.

Who are the spokespersons for this key message?

Think about who will have credibility with the target audiences. Are there language or cultural differences among target audiences? If so, identify different spokespersons for different audiences.

The SOCO worksheet in the appendix may be useful to include in emergency plans or everyday communications.

The right message:

- Is clear, direct, unambiguous
- Includes specific, relevant facts
- Tells people what to do and what to expect

Chapter 6

MISTAKES, MISINFORMATION, AND ALTERNATE FACTS

The concept of The Communications Golden Hour focuses on the importance of having the right steps identified in advance of an emergency *and* thinking through in a meticulous way all the things that could happen—including mistakes. This is a crucial element of emergency planning. In the worst case, people die. In less severe cases, things are just inefficient. In most cases, people just wind up confused.

If a real life-threatening emergency occurs, police or others responsible for emergency management must get a message out rapidly—within 3 to 5 minutes in most instances. However, they also have many other immediate priorities besides communications. This is why turning communications over to a professional communicator—or someone else who is charged specifically with communications—within the initial minutes is every bit as important as dispatching fire engines, ambulances, SWAT teams, or any other emergency responders.

PLAN AND RESPOND WITH THE KNOWLEDGE THAT MISTAKES ARE *ALWAYS* POSSIBLE

A professional communicator needs to immediately confirm that the message already distributed is accurate. The next step is to craft a follow-up message that can be disseminated within no more than 15 to 20 minutes of the onset of the emergency. The first message alerts the public that something is happening. The second provides instructions on what to do. If there were a mistake, the second message can be a rapid retraction.

THINK AHEAD ABOUT HOW TO TALK ABOUT ERRORS BY YOUR AGENCY

Whether an officer-involved shooting, or a video catching someone mistreating a citizen, or anything else, get familiar with the boundary between acknowledging fact and avoiding prejudging something before a proper investigation.

No investigation is needed to conclude that an officer could have done better if video recording shows him berating a citizen who was calmly seated in a restaurant. That does not equal meting out punishment or declaring what led to the situation.

Even in shootings captured on camera, the reasons behind certain facts may be unclear. For example, a video may show that an officer discharged a weapon and that a suspect was struck by bullets and killed. In initial communications, there is no point denying those facts, even though you cannot and should not talk or speculate about *why* this happened.

For example:

"We know from the video that you have all seen that one of our officers discharged a weapon and an individual is deceased. We have begun an investigation to collect all available evidence and determine what led to this."

FIGURE OUT WHERE TO IMPROVE

After every emergency activation, a review (frequently called a "hot wash" or "post mortem") is essential. This is a chance to document the good, the bad, and the really bad. It is an opportunity for team members to share suggestions and recommend changes for the next time.

If anything went wrong, do a root-cause analysis. Trace back to the point where things diverged from what was supposed to happen.

Was there ambiguity? Was there an error? Could it be prevented in the future? What needs to be done now to fix it? This is the same process epidemiologists and detectives follow to investigate outbreaks and crimes. Start with what you know and find the missing facts, then reach a conclusion.

Sadly, there are many examples where communications went wrong, and one always wonders whether lives could have been saved if messages got out better. In Hurricane Katrina, there were many muddled messages, and more than a few instances where people who followed directions wound up in greater peril than if they had ignored them.

COMMON ROOT CAUSES OF MIXED-UP MESSAGING

In addition to word choice and typos, one of the other common sources of confusion is when multiple entities are involved, and their messages are not coordinated. This causes situations like an email message directing people to evacuate a building while a public address announcement in the same building advises people to shelter in place. That happened when there was confusion over jurisdiction—the kind of problem that should not happen during an emergency response.

Even when multiple agencies have jurisdiction, working out communications protocols in advance helps everyone. There is very little good that can come from a situation where a police chief is briefing reporters in one corner and the fire chief is holding a separate briefing at the same time at another corner. Unfortunately, this happens.

The best way to prevent these kinds of problems is to work through them during drills. Practice trusting a mutual aid agency or other responders. If there is a catastrophic emergency, those additional resources may be invaluable—for communications, just as they may be essential for other operational responses.

CORRECT MISINFORMATION—NO MATTER WHERE IT IS FROM

One of the reasons to monitor social media and other news outlets during an emergency is to catch problems fast. If someone with influence puts out incorrect details, get the correct information to that person. In some cases, publish the corrective information directly.

The Boston Police Department took to social media within 10 minutes of the Boston Marathon bombing in 2015, motivated in part by the need to correct wrong information being put out by media outlets and others as the scale of the disaster started to become clear.

In the evening after the Chelsea bombing in New York City in 2016, a politician tweeted that he had been told by the New York City Police Department that "the FBI took several individuals into custody" in connection with the bombing. This was incorrect. The FBI promptly responded to reporters and tweeted out the correct information, without criticizing the politician or anyone else. The FBI message was simply, "We did a traffic stop of a vehicle of interest in the investigation. No one has been charged with any crime. The investigation is continuing."

Names and locations are frequent sources of confusion. When Redwood High School in Larkspur, Calif., was evacuated due to a bomb threat, local media mistakenly reported that the incident was at a different Redwood High School, 40 miles away in Redwood City. This happened even though the initial tweet came from the Central Marin (County) Police.

The media's mistake triggered alarm among parents and others who had no reason for concern. Fortunately, emergency officials and others monitored social media and contacted the outlets that made the mistake, and it was corrected within minutes.

AVOID AMBIGUITY

The Redwood High School confusion is an excellent example of what happens when messages are unintentionally ambiguous. Emergency alerts need to be crafted mindful of possible sources of confusion. Words with multiple meanings are another problem area.

Check location names

Know if there are two places with the same or similar names before you put out your alert and include detail that distinguishes the emergency location to avoid confusion. Even though the originating alert came from a Marin County agency, the tweet itself might have been clearer to a wider audience if it added "in Larkspur."

What went out via Nixle:

> *CENTRAL MARIN PA: Redwood High School is currently in lockdown. Please refer to school notifications system. www.nixle. us/9LE97*

What would have been better:

> *CENTRAL MARIN PA: Redwood HS in Larkspur is currently in lockdown. Please refer to school notifications system. www. nixle.us/9LE97*

Avoid words or phrases with multiple meanings

When a police officer uses the word "investigation," it almost always has criminal implications, yet this word commonly applies to many other situations, many of them entirely benign. Consider whether the public might jump to the wrong conclusion if you use a word that means one thing to you and something else to others.

This is what happened when the owner of the property where Supreme Court Justice Antonin Scalia died in 2016. When he told a reporter that Scalia died with a "pillow over his head," the media and others immediately interpreted that to mean that he had smothered. President Trump even said that the pillow was said to have been found "on his face, which is a pretty unusual place to find a pillow."

It took more than two days for the facts to catch up, with the ranch owner explaining that he meant that the pillow was between Scalia's body and the headboard and "not over his face, as some have been saying."

I found Scalia dead with a pillow over his head: ranch owner

Owner of Texas ranch where Antonin Scalia died clarifies pillow location after 'pillow over his head' comments stir theories

---

REALITY IN THE ERA OF "ALTERNATE FACTS"

One of the most important reasons to begin communicating quickly after an emergency begins is to establish authority, even before solid information is available. By letting media and others know that you are aware of the situation and will have updates, you reduce the chances of someone else taking the stage and conveying misinformation.

This is also where relationships built and maintained over time with media come into play. If reporters see you or your PIO as a straight-shooter, they are more likely to be patient when told that they must wait a few minutes for information.

WHEN THE MEDIA MESSES UP

Reporters make mistakes, like everyone else. Rarely does this happen intentionally, although on occasion, that happens, too. In the case of honest mistakes, contact the reporter directly. In emergency situations, reporters almost always want to be accurate—and cooperative. They see themselves as members of the community, and journalists have a responsibility to convey information that will help keep people away from danger.

This is also why experienced PIOs feel comfortable asking a reporter not to publish certain information. Sometimes, a public message to this effect is appropriate. The Las Vegas Metropolitan Police Department put out a social media message during the initial response to the October 2017 shooting asking people not to share tactical details they may hear on the police scanner. This was an important step, since some individuals and some media were monitoring radio traffic. Reporters or others who were unfamiliar with police radio communications easily could misinterpret what they heard—and potentially publish details that jeopardize the safety of police or others.

If you suspect a deliberate errant story, consider whether to contact their editor. This is risky, as editors are likely to be inclined to back up their people. However, present the facts and avoid judgment. You can avoid responding to certain reporters, but blocking or publicly criticizing them rarely brings good results.

This is also why publishing your own information is essential. Put your briefings on Facebook or Twitter live or post recordings promptly after they are completed. Publish your media statements directly. Give the public access to your information without relying entirely on having it filtered through the news media.

Facts are your friend:

- Get ahead of others so that you establish authority
- Monitor for misinformation. When appropriate, publish corrections—promptly
- Leverage credibility and relationships to push "alternate" voices out of the way

Appendix

TOOLS AND WORKSHEETS

SINGLE OVERRIDING
COMMUNICATIONS OBJECTIVE

What is your key message?

This is the most important point for your audience to understand.

_____

_____

_____

Why is important to convey this message?

What do you want people to do after hearing your message? Why now?

_____

_____

_____

Who needs to hear this message?

Identify your target audience. Are there segments that need different types of attention because of language or other factors?

_____

_____

_____

_____

*Adapted from Single Overriding Communications Objective (SOCO) Work Sheet developed by Bob Howard of the U.S. Centers for Disease Control and Prevention.

What facts support your key message?

Identify at least three convincing details that make your key message believable. Use facts that your target audience will understand, accept, and remember.

_____

_____

_____

Who are the spokespersons for this key message?

Who has credibility with the target audience? Who will they listen to? Who speaks the right language?

_____

_____

_____

DATE: _____

TIME: _____

LOCATION: _____

PREPARED BY: _____

AUTHORIZED BY: _____

CONTACT INFORMATION FOR THE MEDIA:

_____

_____

CONTACT INFORMATION FOR OTHERS:

_____

_____

---

* Adapted from Single Overriding Communications Objective (SOCO) Work Sheet developed by Bob Howard of the U.S. Centers for Disease Control and Prevention.

TACTICAL TOOLS AND LOGISTICS

Advance planning should identify things you know you are going to need no matter what specific emergency occurs. You are going to need phones, spare batteries, paper and pencils, and perhaps a white board or an easel pad. You are probably going to need a camera, and you may need lights or even flashlights. You might need food and water.

You need a place to work. Designate a room or other location and at least one alternate site. Where can staff sleep if the situation goes into multiple days? If your office is inaccessible, where does your team set up shop? In many instances, you can work out a mutual aid agreement with neighboring organizations to cover such eventualities.

What about transportation? Fuel?

What are the essential office supplies and tools?

Each PIO should have their own "go bag" with the items they will need. These are separate from their own personal safety supplies, and each location that may become a communications command center during an emergency should have office and other supplies pre-positioned as well.

A typical PIO "go bag"[1] should include:

- Charged battery pack(s)
- Phone and laptop chargers
- Notepad(s)
- Pens and pencils
- Phone/contact list for key stakeholders
- Phone/contact list for communications personnel
- Copy of emergency protocol
- Maps to designated emergency communications location and alternates

- Hand sanitizer
- Energy bars or other protein-rich snack food
- Toothbrush, toothpaste, mouthwash

Optional but recommended:

- Spare phone
- Mobile hotspot ("MiFi" or the equivalent) device
- PIO safety vest
- Emergency medicine such as Tylenol, Alka-Seltzer, Tums, etc.
- Tea bags, instant coffee, other refreshment
- Spare t-shirt

(Based in part on a presentation by Katie Nelson of the Mountain View Police Department at the International Association of Chiefs of Police annual meeting, 2017)

COMMUNICATIONS EMERGENCY ROLES

Certain tasks need to be handled in every emergency. Depending on the scale of the emergency, designate personnel to perform each of these duties. In some cases, one person can handle multiple tasks.

- **Communications commander**—the person in charge, responsible for all decisions, including personnel assignments.
- **Public information officer**—this is the person who speaks to the public or the media in the emergency and is responsible for crafting messages for review and approval by the Communications Commander and other authorities, as required by your protocols.
- **Liaison**—this person is the connection between the communications team and the incident command center. Designating a single person responsible for this duty is essential to orderly communications during an emergency, when activities can—and should—move quickly.

- **Listener (or Monitor)**—closely follows news media and social media to determine whether your key messages are being reported, to identify inaccurate coverage, and to gather information about the emergency from other sources.

- **Scribe**—maintains a chronological log of major activities by the communications team during the emergency, including arrival and departure of personnel and interactions with the news media or public. Also maintains official record of public statements, including time and method of release for each.

MAJOR INCIDENT COMMUNICATIONS CHECKLIST

If there is an imminent or ongoing public safety risk:

- Disseminate very brief alert message via all available channels.
- Activate PIO or designate acting PIO.

Follow promptly with:

- Advisory on where to go for updates, more details, and when to expect them.
- Caution for people not to share unconfirmed information.
- Realistic update schedule; promise only what you can deliver.

Establish media staging area and schedule for briefings:

- Make sure it is outside of potential danger zone.
- Use space that is under your control whenever possible (HQ).
- Log media inquiries, including contact info for each reporter.

Keep to promised schedule, even if updates are simply "nothing new to report."

MEDIA BRIEFING TIPS

- Determine your spokesperson.

Should be a senior official but does not have to be the incident commander or chief. In a working incident, consider whether IC should stay focused on incident command and have an alternate authority as the briefer. Similarly, hospitals should avoid taking physician out of emergency department if they are needed for patient care.

Spokesperson should wear what they wear to work. Important to look professional but not too different from other emergency responders.

- Determine your Single Overriding Communications Objective.
- Give people a clear call to action.

If nothing else, point them to online or other resources for education/information/crime tip hotline, etc.

- Designate a safe place for media to set up.
- Be mindful that incidents can change or grow.
- Designate the time for each briefing.
- Have support staff available to log names and contact info of media present and keep track of questions asked.
- At end of briefing, indicate when next briefing will occur.

COMMUNICATIONS CHANNELS

Every agency has different channels available for emergency communications. Most have several, and some are part of municipal or other multi-agency systems. These are in addition to traditional methods, such as telephone, email, door-to-door, news conferences, and public meetings.

Determining which methods are appropriate for emergencies depends on the nature of the emergency and each community's characteristics.

Social media

Twitter—The place where media and others usually go first for immediate information

Facebook—Social sharing, easy-to-use live video to agency pages; works best if audience is directed to visit specific page.

Instagram—Fast, easy sharing of photos or other visual information

Snapchat—Popular among younger people, used for videos that are not searchable or stored

Pinterest—Powerful search capability, primarily for visual information, not breaking news

LinkedIn—Business oriented, not widely seen as source for breaking news

NextDoor—Social sharing site geared toward neighborhood sharing. Use varies widely from community to community.

Emergency Alert Systems

Most of these work with the federal system that can push emergency messages across multiple regional alert systems, including radio and television and cell phones, in addition to serving as routine warning systems for lesser emergencies. Specific capabilities vary.

AlertSense
AmberAlertGPS – LEAP (Law Enforcement Alerting Portal)
Asher Group – Hyper Reach
AtHoc – IWS Alerts
Blackboard – Blackboard Connect
Buffalo Computer Graphics – DisasterLAN
Comlabs – EMNet
CommPower – iNotify
Everbridge – Nixle
Federal Signal Corporation – CenterPoint Dashboard
Geo-Comm, Inc. – GeoLynx
GSS Alert Studio – ALERT FM
HipLink
Inspiron Logistics – WENS
Intermedix – WebEOC
Interop-Solutions – Paraclete
KDEE Technology LLC – On-the-go Alerting
Monroe Electronics – DAS-EOC
NC4 – E-Team
OnSolve – CodeRED
Ping 4 – Ping 4 Alerts!
egroup Mass Notifications – CivicPlus
SwiftReach – Swift911
Rave Mobile Safety - Rave Alert

PLANNING FOR EXTENDED INCIDENTS

After an initial emergency response, public information messages should get longer, with more detail, including guidance for post-incident recovery. When will streets reopen? When can people return? What happened? Sometimes an update that simply says "there is no new information" can be reassuring.

As with all public information messages, accuracy and credibility are vital, so report information quickly and completely. If errors occur, correct them immediately. Give people directions on where to turn or who to call for more information.

Every emergency communications plan should include a staffing plan for long-duration emergencies. If indications are that an incident will extend beyond one shift, identify and alert second shift personnel at the earliest point possible, but do not bring them on-duty early—they need to rest up and be fresh when the first shift fades.

After the first hour (if not already done or in-progress):

1. A communications officer other than the person at the emergency operations center should be at the field command post to manage any on-site media, and report conditions back to communications commander (ongoing).
2. Determine potential need for additional personnel or other resources to field incoming inquiries. Are there families trying to track down missing persons? Is a call center needed? If so, how can it be activated?
3. Coordinate with hospital communicators, coroner and other agencies.

After four hours:

1. Prepare and send update to community. If warranted, craft specific messages for different segments, but make sure facts are consistent.

2. If media gathering, establish staging location if not done already. Provide logistical support (power, refreshments, etc.).
3. Determine need for media briefing or media site tours. Set time and location. Set up to transmit via Facebook, Twitter, or YouTube live, if possible.

After eight hours:

1. If incident was covered by news media, conduct an update briefing or issue updated advisory.
2. Determine need for ongoing operations. Plan for food and supplies. Contact backup PIOs/writers from other agencies if necessary.
3. Direct staff what to do about normal work.

If duration exceeds 24 hours:

1. Implement staffing plan, account for logistics such as transportation, food, shelter.
2. Determine regular briefing schedule. In most situations, there should be a minimum of two briefings each day—one in the early morning and another before the evening newscasts. In rapidly changing situations, briefings should be more frequent, such as every four hours or more. Briefings are the best way to organize a flood of inbound media requests.
3. If possible, implement "longer form" communications tools, such as produced videos or clips that can be distributed to the media.
4. Communicate your briefing plans to the media. Update as needed.

Adapted in part from materials originally developed at the University of California

ABOUT THE AUTHOR

Few people have been in the middle of as many front-page breaking stories like Doug Levy. Trained as a lawyer, Levy is an award-winning journalist and advises public safety agencies, health departments, universities, hospitals, and police departments on how to get emergency messages out when lives are on the line. Levy was among the first people to embrace social media as an emergency communications tool.

He was chief communications officer at Columbia University Medical Center in New York from 2010 to 2015. As director of communications and lecturer at the University of California, San Francisco School of Medicine from 2004-2009, Levy worked closely with the university police department to transform emergency planning and communications.

Levy was a reporter for USA Today in the 1990s. He worked at National Public Radio, United Press International, and the Mutual Broadcasting System/NBC Radio Network News.

He was Firefighter II and EMT in Howard County, Md., for nine years and president of the Savage, Md., Volunteer Fire Company. From 2013-2017, he was a community relations volunteer with NYPD.

Levy holds a law degree from the University of Maryland, a master's in journalism from Northwestern University, and a bachelor's in history from the University of California. He is admitted to the Maryland Bar, on inactive status.

More information is available at douglevy.com.

CUSTOM TRAINING FOR YOUR ORGANIZATION

With experience as a firefighter, EMT, award-winning journalist and communications leader, few others can match Doug Levy's record of cool, clear thinking when others are scrambling.

Now, you can apply Doug's methods to plan, prepare, practice and perfect your emergency communications plans.

"Great workshop"

"Interactive and thoughtprovoking"

WORKSHOPS INCLUDE:

"(Doug) pushed participants to think past their immediate responses."

• Who people trust
• How to get people to act
• Effective message crafting

ALL WORKSHOPS LED BY EXPERIENCED PUBLIC SAFETY COMMUNICATORS.

"I feel much more confident in being able to handle an emergency activation."

STREAMLINE YOUR EMERGENCY COMMUNICATIONS INCLUDE:

Major injury survival changed when the importance of the first 60 minutes was recognized and trauma care was streamlined around that golden hour. Communications decisions in the first 60 minutes of an emergency are similarly critical.

Based on his book and 30 years of experience, Levy shows how to plan, prepare, and practice. Workshops are interactive, dynamic, and tailored to your needs.

SCHEDULE YOUR FREE
CONSULTATION
TODAY AT
DOUGLEVY.COM

CPSIA information can be obtained
at www.ICGtesting.com
Printed in the USA
LVHW070425070623
749020LV00006B/228

9 781732 065901